# MOVIE TECHNIQUES FOR THE ADVANCED AMATEUR

By George Régnier
with additional material
by Myron A. Matzkin

Translated from "Construire Un Film," with the authorization
of Publications Photo Et Cinéma Paul Montel—Paris

Translation by Nadine Dormoy Savage
New York

American Photographic Book Publishing Co. Inc.
33 West 60th Street     New York 23, N.Y.

# Contents

CHAPTER 1

# Amateur Movie Making

The amateur movie maker may occasionally feel that there is a great chasm between himself and the professional cinematographer—when in reality the only division is one of misunderstanding. The professional does not look at the amateur's efforts with a condescending eye—if only for the reason that no one who genuinely loves cinema indulges in such an attitude. The professional is vitally interested in amateur films if only for the obvious fact that the amateur filmer is by definition a lover of motion pictures and therefore a friend of the professional.

Amateur, or home movie making has grown tremendously, both in 8 and 16mm, in the last few years. Literally millions of people own motion picture cameras. Clubs dedicated to making motion pictures have become numerous—and constructive. Amateur motion pictures have increased in quality and originality to the point where they often compare to and even surpass professionally-made films. The amateur film festival, in Cannes, France, for example, has become a legitimately important international event. The idea of the film festival has grown in the United States, where we have the Photographic Society of America Ten Best awards, the Ten Best of the West, an annual competition held in Louisville, Kentucky, and several other more local competitions and screenings. Many amateurs have become excellent professionals—producing and photographing exceptional films in the theatrical, travel, scientific, exploratory, medical, and technical fields.

Many of the outstanding productions featured at the various film societies sprinkled throughout the country are the work of either amateurs or men and women who can at best be called semi-professionals.

But not all amateurs aspire to professional status. Some never acquire the slickness, the skill, or the attitude required for making money from movies. And, every day there are more amateurs who are simply attracted by the fascinating business of recording action on a length of film. The purpose of this book is to present the techniques and experience gained in my years as a professional—explaining and applying the basic methods that work for both the amateur and the professional. For after all, both start out with a camera, film and an idea—and everything else to a great extent depends on the imagination and creative drive of the individual. It is my hope that this book will not only contribute to the enjoyment of making motion pictures—but also in seeing them.

## Amateur and Professional Motion Pictures

In one sense at least it has been almost impossible to apply mass production techniques and standards to motion pictures. You just can't successfully mass produce fantasy in the way automobiles, refrigerators, or washing machines come off an assembly line. You can't vary the emotional impact of a single motion picture to give it a different look, as one can change the color of an automobile to make it look slightly different from a neighbor's. Films just don't come in several models and color combinations—romantic blue or sexy pink or ocean green. Each film stands by itself—good, bad or mediocre. It stands alone even when it follows a tried and true pattern.

And every time the dream merchants of the major studios around the world become complacent you can almost bet that someone with an outdated camera and just enough money for film will turn out a superlative, imaginative, meaningful film.

And this is where the amateur and professional find the real meaning of their kinship. The amateur has the freedom to work as he pleases—whether shooting a roll of 8mm film on his front lawn or chasing a much more ambitious film concept.

Perhaps the man closest to the amateur is the producer and cinematographer working on the documentary motion picture. While the documentary can be a film showing nothing more than the endless production line of a can factory, or packing and loading crackers, it can also be the fantastically beautiful films of Robert Flaherty, Joris Ivens, Marcel Ichac, or Arne Suksdorf.

The documentary film maker constantly seeks the new, the different, the unknown—either at his door step, or in the world around him, like Roman Vischniac, or in some vague outland. The documentary team is small—usually no more than two or three technicians—people with a do-it-yourself attitude, modest or even scant financial resources. Their films cannot be costly and the conditions under which they work are quite similar to those of the amateur. The amateur has one thing that quite often even the documentarian does not—complete freedom to shoot as he chooses. The amateur makes his own decisions without consulting anyone. He has the freedom to make mistakes. The amateur and professional may use a different film width, but both are irrevocably motion picture makers. What counts is the know-how. That's what the following pages are about. But first, let's take a quick look at what its like to be a non-professional.

## The Tools: Research, Imagination

There is no real definition of amateur movie making. One is not an amateur film maker in quite the same way that one is an amateur athlete or a stamp collector. One definition of amateur states that he must not make his living from photography or movie making—but can earn part of his income that way. But an amateur may be someone who works for a camera manufacturer or who shoots still pictures professionally but not motion pictures. He may sell equipment over a counter—or he may work on a studio lot as an electrician or a script writer, or an actor. Or he may be a school teacher, a millionaire, a doctor, baker,

8

THE GOLD RUSH. — Charlie Chaplin (1925).—This picture from "The Gold Rush" summarizes perfectly the simplicity of technique used by Chaplin, the comparison of the human quality of his character with the sympathy he arouses. Note his concern for the right expressive detail—for example the tablecloth made out of a naively cut newspaper. Such a detail goes unnoticed on the screen, since attention is concentrated on the actor. (Photo: United Artists)

lawyer, Indian chief—just about anyone with a camera who uses it.

But the amateur goes through a metamorphosis—which starts the first day he picks up a movie camera from the counter at his local photo shop. He is vaguely afraid—particularly of getting mixed up with what he may call tricks. He only knows that his friend or neighbor has successfully exposed several rolls or magazines of film. Our amateur may even be a bit afraid of this complicated machine in his hand. But if he thinks about it at all, it occurs to him that getting an image on movie film is really no more difficult than getting one on a single negative in a still camera.

Equipment? Nothing more than a camera, projector, perhaps a tripod and an exposure meter. After a while—and a quick reading of the manual that came with the camera—our amateur starts shooting. It's really not difficult at all. His first films look great—the first time he sees them. Then he begins to notice all the errors of exposure, framing, panning, and perhaps even a few things that are original with him alone.

But as he keeps exposing more film his technique gets better. Exposure, panning, and all the rest are by now at least satisfactory. He may even take a crack at producing a slightly ambitious movie—and he just may not be up to it. He goes back to making less taxing films, knowing that as he gains experience he'll climb back to the heights he tried for rather unsuccessfully.

But let's not get the idea that the world of the amateur is limited. The possibilities for non-professional films are almost infinite. Actually, there are so many ways of linking together a series of images, of establishing a filmic rhythm, of projecting a meaning, that there is no boundary that the amateur can't cross—in time.

But the amateur must know his equipment, learn constantly from experience and then evaluate his own capabilities. Just what kinds of films can the amateur shoot? Generally speaking, the kinds of films that the amateur is most apt to tackle can be classified under three general headings:

> Recording of personal events
> Documentary
> The story telling film

These headings are arbitrary and can be further subdivided in many categories —some of which cannot be easily differentiated from each other. The headings are flexible enough to overlap constantly. For example, under recording of personal events one can certainly include travelogues—which are as a rule considered documentaries. And in filming a documentary, one might inter-weave a story for continuity. So let's not be too concerned with labels but rather with what an amateur can produce.

## The Recording of Personal Events

Without much doubt, the first thing the amateur is liable to try will be the recording of personal events. Often, this is the motivation for buying a motion picture camera in the first place. It's a pleasant thing to re-experience through film the moments in life that were particularly important or happy. Actually, personal film making is something like the family album many of our parents kept on the mantle—a book that might be filled with snapshots of dignified gentlemen with beards, and ladies with flounced skirts staring into the lens.

But the modern movie camera makes it possible to give movement and dimension to the family album—keeping alive the image of familiar faces, what someday may be the "old" family car, and figures and memories we hold dear.

## Making the Film of Personal Events

This kind of film definitely does not require elaborate techniques—and usually sharp, well framed images are sufficient. But just as there was a logic to the sequence of snapshots in the old family album, the personal film should have a certain continuity. This makes them more enjoyable—and often more appealing. A film should be more than just a series of animated images flashing briefly on a screen—recorded here and there by chance. Whether or not we are conscious of it, the events in our personal films have a logical sequence and tend to be related. Let's take the family dinner—something that may happen in your family quite often. It has an organized framework and because of that can be related as a story. The same order applies to making a film. If the order is followed we avoid repetition and overlong sequences.

FILMS WITH CHILDREN. — When faced with these truly candid actors, the camera must be unobtrusive and the cameraman alert.

1. Peter is not concerned with the camera, he's only interested in persuading his brother to play with him.

4. Pat finally agrees to take part in the game and he seriously shows how to do it. The children are too busy playing to pay any attention to the movements of the cameraman. They can be shot on a very tight frame.

2. We have backed up quickly in order to get both children in the frame. Pat, the older brother, takes a slightly condescending look at the unsatisfactory technique of Peter.

5. Naturally, Peter immediately demolishes the sand pile. (We come closer and change the angle slightly in order to look closer at this act of vandalism).

3. "Gosh! He can't do it right! Who makes a sand pile like that!" (a longer lens makes it possible to isolate Pat in a close-up, while he looks at his brother).

6. Pat (again, a close-up on him) complains loudly.

**7.** Things are taking a bad turn. Before we have to separate the fighters, we may still have time and the necessary speed pan quickly (the photo indicates where the pan starts and where it ends) to the sudden offensive of Peter and the shovel full of sand which he throws in his brother's face.
*(Photos by Jacques Boulas)*

But this attention to making a movie that has an essential form doesn't mean we stifle the spontaneity of what we are filming. Unless we avoid "directing" we may spoil the chances for preserving a living memory. Actually, people in our personal films should be unaware of the camera. Avoid the posed, stilted artificial film so that your movies will have a feeling of reality—of life itself. Much of what will be said in the following pages can be applied to the personal film—not only from the point of view of pure technique but in respect to the general principles of good film making.

## The Travelogue

The travelogue is one of the more prevalent subjects of the amateur motion picture maker. The camera serves to record images we see only briefly—and may forget even more quickly. As I have already mentioned, the personal film and the travelogue often resemble each other. However, the travelogue, if it is to be successful, requires careful planning.

A travelogue deals with a change in time and space, the basis for motion pictures generally. To plan our film so that it will be an interesting, accurate account of a trip we must make the correct selection of images and avoid repetition. Otherwise we may find ourselves involved in making a much longer film than originally planned. For one thing, we must decide that just having

STATIC SUBJECTS. — From a trip to Venice, it's only natural that you should want movies of magnificent landmarks, such as the San Marco Cathedral above, whose exuberant ornamentation suggests innumerable angles for the camera.

one pleasant scene follow another isn't enough. As in still photography, good taste, and the avoidance of the cliche and the banal are important. Colored post cards, even if they move, can be rather boring.

## How to Shoot a Travelogue

You probably won't find it necessary to get involved with script writing for your travelogue. Besides, you'll probably decide that creating a script about a place you may have never seen is rather impossible. Actually, the unexpected and the unpredictable make a trip exciting and amateurs can hardly be expected to make the preshooting trip that professionals often find necessary. However, even if you can't establish in advance the contents of your film, establish them as you go along. As you travel, take one shot in order to introduce a second, shift the camera angle for greater visual interest, and always keep in mind the order of each scene. Putting the entire film together will be easier when you finally sit down to your editing bench.

Let's suppose that while driving on a strange road you come upon a breathtaking view. You decide to film it. The obvious way would be to run off a few feet of film and drive on. Instead, you might turn the car around, and film the road to the spectacular vista as you drive back toward it. Then, as you stop near the view again, you have someone drive the car to precisely the spot where you first discovered the scene. You shoot the car coming to a halt and the driver

**LIVING IMAGES.** — The cinema is movement. Let's not neglect—in spite of all the beautiful architecture—to record living images; a street scene, interesting people, such as for instance these seed sellers who receive free advertising among the tourists because of the famous pigeons.

*(Photos by Georges Régnier)*

steps out. You change the angle again and shoot the scenery. Now you've got a meaningful sequence.

In shooting your travelogue, beware of exposing too much film of monuments or other static subjects. It might be a good idea to avoid following the example of some of the theatrically released documentaries as a model for your movie.

While it may be that the monuments and other historically interesting features of a locale were the reason for your trip, remember that the total impression is the best way to show your enjoyment of it. Sometimes, the recording of fleeting details, faces, unusual discoveries and odd bits of movement and life gives the really true picture.

Let's say that after you show the monumental proportions of a Gothic church, you film the horse and carriage that passes by, or the woman who sells ice cream behind a stand. Forget the scenery in its grander aspects for a moment, and film a close-up of the guide telling a story to an old lady who doesn't comprehend one word he says.

You'll be surprised when you edit your movie how these "little" shots add life and rhythm to your film. Your camera is an eye, make sure it sees everything.

### The Documentary Film

The documentary film is closely related to the travelogue. While the films

1. Take advantage of the excitement when everybody is going on board to introduce the background with your camera: the ship and the unsuspecting actors.

2. The car which the derrick is lifting in the air—which your camera has followed by panning up—can be used as a good introduction to the ship itself.

3. This old woman is much too interested by the movement around her to notice that your camera is on her. Here is a flash (that is, a very short scene), full of color.

4. From the deck you can take this high angle view which can be framed easily: the net is seen in diagonal, as are the pavements of the dock. At the opposite angle, on the upper right, is the figure of a man, creating an interesting composition.

5. The boat is on its way, the harbor recedes in the distance. Here's a self-made dolly shot you don't want to miss. The objects in the foreground and the passengers in the middle ground emphasize the movement away from the land.

6. The action of this sailor mooring the ship is an excellent transition between scenes of the cruise and those of the scenes when docking.

(*Photos by Jacques Boulas*)

15

that confine themselves to a study of button manufacture or petroleum refining are best left strictly within the province of the professional, the documentary has many possibilities. There's often a penchant for labeling the short subject, one kind of documentary we see fairly often at the local movie, as a bore. But the documentary has gone through a renaissance. Occasionally, we may see one that's well done. Actually, the documentarian's task is to search out the meaning of the arts, relationships of people, and the color and background of nations. Even when the subject is an industrial one, the approach should be more human than an objective study of efficient mechanical design.

The documentary requires patience, invention and ingenuity—and compared to the fantastic budgets of the feature film, survives on a pauper's subsistence.

## Documentary Subjects

The documentary film, if it is to be interesting, must concern itself with a subject that permits sticking to truth without embellishment or fiction. For example, you may decide that the pretty little village you spend your summers in would make an interesting documentary. So you attempt to capture the intrinsic values of this village—the ones that make it different from other places. You shoot at dawn—catching the rising sun, the rooster's cry. You show the commonplace activities of the village. You film the lengthening shadows of evening and the lights going on in the windows all over the village. Your film is the expression of a peaceful day in the country—and has a unity in time and place. Its form is simple, direct—and appealing.

Or, you can probe under the surface of the town, letting your film tell the reasons and forces that shape its existence. Your film delves into history, as shown by old, scarred walls, winding streets, ancient buildings, and almost forgotten customs. The library supplies you with some of the background you need. Townspeople fill in the gaps.

But the danger here is that you will go overboard on monuments—things of the past—and forget the living. Your film may be nothing more than an endless series of shots that could easily be duplicated on a series of slides. So, you provide movement and people. The sparkling water of the fountain may have a counterpoint in the people who use it. Or, the old wall may be a child's key to the world of make believe—and this becomes part of your film, too.

Another documentary may be about a river, showing the lands it goes through. Local industry, a construction job, a harbor, the street on which you live, the work of a local group, a landmark that will soon disappear (the Third Avenue L, in New York, for example), even manhole covers, can be documentary material. Anything that has to do with living and people can be filmed in the documentary style. You may not discover anything new—but the element that will make your film different is you, and how you approach your subject.

## The Newsreel

The newsreel film, whether amateur or professional, is often both a documentary and a travelogue. The news film implies giving your audience a quick

AN ISLAND IN THE SUN. — The harbor, the people, the colorful costumes call for a camera.

1. The appearance of a small boat provides an opportunity for a following shot which discovers the town built on the side of a hill

4. Here the white facades act as reflectors and create very light shadow areas which will not hide the detail.

2. A marketplace: shades, shapes and light—colors too. The sharp contrast between the dark and the bright areas create a few problems with exposure. Expose for shadow detail, but avoid large areas of highlight in the background.

5. Here, on the contrary, we have highlights with only a little contrasting shadow. The whiteness is emphasized by the open door and by the two women dressed in black. There's hardly any color in the scene.

3. There's a picturesque colleague: Let's not miss the humorous things.

6. On the other hand, these women wearing their Sunday best make for a very colorful scene. Shoot unobtrusively when you can to capture things as they really are.

(*Photos by Jacques Boulas*)

**HIGH PASTURES. — Here is a subject which makes both a report and a documentary.**

1. Extreme wide-angle shots convey the atmosphere of this continuous flow of sheep on the move in rocky and bare country.

2. A medium shot follows the march of the billy-goat who, wearing a bell, leads the way.

5. Let's take a look inside. The light that comes through the door brings the rustic room to life.

6. Sidelight hits this scene. The shadow of a tree stands out on the mountain side while the flock enjoys the grass.

9. Against the gray background of the mountain, dark and light silhouettes stand out in this medium long shot.

10. The flock comes for water. Here's a chance to come closer to the timid ewes and the violent rams.

18

**3.** The old shepherd comes forward, then stops a while in close-up, looking straight ahead at some mountain top.

**4.** A pan starts on the snow-covered mountain top, follows the rocky mountain side and ends on the shepherd's shanty.

**7.** The hungry lambs make a wonderful close-up shot.

**8.** The distribution of salt brings the sheep in one big flock. The backlighting enhances the coats of the sheep.

**11.** The images in the film are diversified as stillness and movement alternate on the scene in long shots or close-ups.

**12.** "The flock, like a lake, sprawls around, splashes a while, then falls asleep" (Jean Giono).

(*Photos by Jacques Boulas*)

19

look at life—without applying makeup or pretention. It's the kind of film that records an act that cannot be duplicated, an exciting moment. It may be nothing more than a baby going for its first stroll—or something like a football player scoring a winning touchdown. The professional newsreel makes you a participant in the world's events. You may see it in the movies well after the event or on TV at the moment it takes place.

The professional, operating with highly portable equipment, devotes much of his ability to being at the right place at the right time. He doesn't worry about technical refinements, sacrificing the fine points of image to getting the image in the first place.

The newsreel cameraman may be his own director. He may select the image, relate it to other shots, and exercise his own judgment in many other instances. He is, in a large sense, closely related to the amateur. I've elaborated to some extent on the newsreel cameraman to show the special qualities this kind of man must have. He shoots a variety of films that actually fit within the scope of the amateur.

### Newsreel Subjects

The newsreel film, even shot on an amateur plane, suggests a wide range of subject matter. If action is your dish, you can try your hand (and your camera) at sports filming. In most cases, you'll have to arrange for a good deal of freedom inside the arena. That may be easy for the professional, but an amateur usually has to apply some fast, convincing talk to the situation. Sports filming means getting close to the action, overriding official objections, and even taking a chance on arousing the crowd to get the best footage.

But if sports, except on a local level, seem a bit far afield, there are many other areas for the amateur news-type film. If you've got sea legs, you might try shooting a fishing trip—either on a sports or commercial boat. In fact, anything from mountain climbing to a local fair makes good newsreel footage. A little imagination, and a dash of the Rene Claire technique for humor, and you have an interesting film.

A city offers many opportunities for the report, or newsreel, film—boat rides, walks in the various parks, or even traffic jams. Whatever you choose, you'll need a quick eye, good reflexes and a sense of being on a hunt—a hunt for good film.

### The Scripted Film

Finally, there is the film that tells a story—with planned scenes and actors. You made some rather good films while traveling or on vacation. But you want to do more than record life. You want to compose it in your own way—to tell a story. The ideas or images may already be in your mind. This is where motion pictures can become a consuming interest—even terribly demanding. But it is also more ambitious than other types of filming.

Images must be linked together and each one a meaningful piece that fits precisely with the one that comes before and the one that comes afterward. Every scene is dependent on the others. You can no longer take chances, hoping for the best. Shooting problems will be more complex. Work will have to be

LES HALLES, PARIS. — An open air market is a good documentary subject.

1. This oblique ray of light occupies a good portion of the street lengthwise. The coming and going of laborers, of vehicles, of buyers, make a continuous ballet of silhouettes as in a magic lantern.

4. There are plenty of picturesque figures in the crowd, and behind the various baskets and boxes there are excellent hiding places for the cameraman who doesn't want to be seen.

2. A lively street seller addresses us directly. Her movement and her expression aimed directly at the lens are very valuable in a documentary.

5. The loading of a hand truck can be filmed first with a close-up, followed with a pan shot as it moves.

3. Farther off, another lady is too busy praising her merchandise to notice the slight noise of the camera.

6. This "still picture" could be used as a finale and a background for your title: "The end".

(*Photos by Jacques Boulas*)

organized and a logical procedure followed in film production—in the idea, script, sequences, editing, shooting, and sound.

## The Film and Its Creator

To meet the problems of making a film based on a script you'll need a certain amount of experience. I've mentioned that like other arts, the motion picture depends on imagination. It follows no absolute rules except when dealing with purely technical problems. There are no precise answers for each situation. Since you'll rarely find two given situations completely the same, you'll have to create answers each time. You'll learn a few tricks, ways to solve problems, acquire experience that will prevent mistakes, and become familiar with rules (where rules apply). But with all that, you'll be strictly on your own.

Your own taste will dictate answers modified by imagination, temperament and sensitivity. Otherwise factors that should have a tight rein on them will get out of control; light, movement, time, faces, actor's reactions.

And there are always several films in the one film you produce. First, there is the film as it appears on paper. Each scene is carefully planned and corresponds to a number in the script. This is the ideal film—the one that you will never produce.

Then, there's the film that will be made. That's the one you will build piece by piece, using concrete materials this time, not just words. Real things don't yield to your wishes. In fact, they tend to resist them and that's why your thinking must to a certain extent adapt itself to reality. The production of your film may appear to you as a series of concessions—a succession of minor defeats.

Third, we have the completely photographed film—not yet edited. Actually, it's a confused succession of images, scenes—a film that seems a stranger to your original idea. But as you edit a new film comes to life. While it may not be what you wanted it to be, here and there you see some of the things you tried to do. You make an effort to capture the complete idea again—tying together threads which were broken. Now the main idea appears. You purify it—staying with it by cutting, throwing away much footage, and linking images. Then, if you have been honest with yourself—not taken the easy way out—and stayed as close as possible to the original idea, the film comes to life. It may not be the exact film you dreamed about—but it comes fairly close and takes the place of the dream. You begin to like it.

## Production Teams

Many production teams have been created within amateur groups—and a good idea, too. Motion pictures are essentially based on teamwork. A collaborator may bring skills which you do not possess—and help to express your ideas. One may be a technician and another an idea man. Even though the personality of a director is the most obviously expressed thing in many professional films—the picture is usually the result of teamwork. Many people worked on the script besides the producer; the author, the script writer, the adapter, and the director. The director works closely with soundmen, the cameraman, costume designers, music composers, lab technicians, and the editor. A great film is above all the creation of one man who is capable of channeling various talents and activities toward one goal.

If you have a production team at all, it will be small. But attempt to make each one's job understood. While it's a good idea to have as many as possible work on a film, a job needs a foreman. That's you.

### What Makes a Fiction Film?

It's almost impossible to define the precise boundaries for the fiction, or theatrical film. This is one kind of motion picture that obviously defies rules or specific definitions. Here we are, faced with an art form that has almost unlimited flexibility as far as technique. Marcel L'Herbier, one of the great screen writers, said that no subject was impossible and even an essay on law could be adapted to motion pictures. While the statement wasn't completely serious, just about anything can be expressed cinematographically.

At the start of your theatrical film making it might be wise to stick to extremely simple stories—particularly if you haven't acquired script writing experience. But this isn't just a piece of advice that one hands to amateurs— simply because they are amateurs. Even in professional film making some of the best movies have been made around stories that could be summarized in a few lines. In any event, your own taste, background, and temperament will dictate your direction. A film is a mirror of the kind of person who makes it— and following your natural bent will best reflect your personality.

You may prefer action, or a film with force and drama. Then again, your creative instincts may tend toward the poetic or even the humorous.

The actual creation of a story for a motion picture can be rather trying. But first attempt to find a solid basis for your story. It may have its roots in an item in the newspapers, a short story you read, or perhaps something that you actually experienced. There are, for example, any number of solid classical and modern short stories that are good film material. But there are film possibilities in poems, orchestral music, even songs. But whatever you choose as a beginning, it will serve as a springboard and a guide to your own imagination.

### Freedom of the Amateur Film

The really great thing about working as an amateur is the wonderful freedom from all kinds of restraints—public opinion, censorship (both moralistic and the kind that stems from considerations of saleability), and the need to make money.

This is the kind of freedom that professional movie makers just don't have— and for which they envy the amateur. It means that the amateur can approach film making with an eye for the original, with a disregard for the stereotype. He can travel a straight road to creating the unusual, even the poetic.

But this doesn't mean that you, as an amateur should depart from the path of logic and delve completely into the area of the abstract. Somehow, you must communicate ideas. However, as long as you maintain a rapport with your audience, you have a freedom that the "dream merchants" can never attain. Between the paid artist and his dreams always lies the need to make money for himself—or someone else. You, as an amateur, control the film from inception to completion. But to be successful, to project an idea, you've got to acquire the facility that only the mastering of technique can give you.

## Film and Its Technicians

Before we jump into the question of "how does one make a film?" we ought to ask one other question: What is film made of?

Most of the answers are true for amateur and professional alike. A film depends on its means of production—which in turn depends on budget. Or, in the simplest possible terms—how much you can afford.

1. *Film size.* You'll have to choose between 8 and 16mm. Costs—and often results—are different with both widths. The width you select will also determine to some extent the camera, projector and other equipment you buy.

2. *Camera.* Whether you choose an 8 or 16mm, motion picture cameras range from the simplest box-type units to complex machines that can do almost any film job.

3. *Black-and-white or color.* Here again money enters the picture—but doesn't necessarily dictate the entire decision. You'll have to think about the film speed you need—and the artistic appropriateness of either black-and-white or color to what you are shooting.

4. *Time.* Perhaps the most difficult item for the amateur to get is the time to make his film. The abundance or lack of time plays an important role in every decision you make.

After you've solved some of the above-mentioned factors, have roughed out a shooting script, and studied your subject, there comes a new set of problems and decisions. These have to do with actual production.

1. *Technique:* Framing, camera movements, angle, transitions, order of sequences.

2. *Background:* The choice and use you'll make of your shooting location.

3. *Actors:* The search for characterization, direction (and even makeup if needed).

Shooting conditions bring a third set of problems, depending on location.

1. *Exteriors:* daylight

2. *Interiors:* artificial light

3. *Film:* Really related to the first set of decisions—but something that recurs everytime you make a film.

Then, of course, you'll have to think about special effects—fades, dissolves, superimpositions and slow motion and other fps variations. You may do some special effects in the camera—opticals mainly—or add them in the editing stage. So you solve some of the technical problems as a cameraman, others as an editor—and then face the matter of sound. The sum of all these decisions will be your film.

Don't be frightened by what appears to be a never ending cycle of decisions. These separate items are linked together in a definite order and relationship. You should be aware of—but not stymied—by them. The flexibility of modern amateur equipment provides many of the solutions you'll need. Taking things as they come, actually playing the various roles of producer, script writer, director, cameraman, editor and sound man, in proper sequence provides the rest of the answers.

24

CHAPTER 2

# You Are the Producer

What part does the producer play in making a professional motion picture? Actually, he's the man who organizes the film and makes many, if not all the key decisions—subject, script writer, actors, technicians. He, if he is to be successful, he must bring discrimination, judgment and good sense to the office every day. And, in the final analysis, he's got to be a little lucky. Unlike the man who makes automobiles or dish washers, the producer sells one item—entertainment. He's selling something whose real value is elusive and at the same time real—but often totally defies definition. While the professional producer's big worry can be defined in terms of money, you as an amateur aren't concerned with profit. Still, motion pictures, even those that deal with baby's first steps, cost money. Let's take a look at some of the material you'll need to make films.

## Film Size

One of the least informative ways to get information on which film size—8 or 16mm—is best for you is to ask a faithful user of one or the other. Either film maker can give you dozens of reasons why one is better—and often they'll use the same words.

A good many words have already been written about the subject, but there are some facts that might help you make a decision. First let's look at 8mm.

The smaller gauge film costs less than 16mm. Properly handled, it provides a darn good image. Sure, it has its limitations. You can't project a really large screen image with 8mm. Maximum screen size, under really ideal conditions, is about 7 feet on the horizontal. If you plan to show your films to limited audiences that won't be a factor.

However, if you're definitely after professional quality and flexibility, 16mm is a must. Also, if you intend to make your film commercially available, you'll have to use 16mm. Even large screen projection in a full size auditorium is possible with 16mm. But 16mm is more expensive.

However, if film making is brand new to you, you may want to start with 8mm and make your early mistakes in the least costly manner possible. Later, as you get a better grip on technique, you can graduate to 16mm—although hardly anyone I know likes to replace equipment.

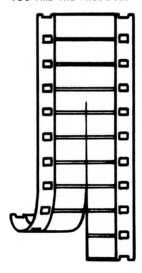
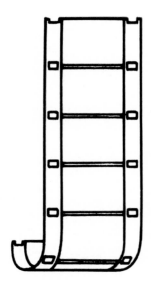

SIZES (from left to right). — 8mm. The type for the recording of personal events. It is actually 16mm film. Both sides are run through the camera. The film is slit lengthwise after it is developed. 16mm. because of its picture quality and the possibilities of sound, this film is the preferred type of film of amateurs and many professionals. However, cost is higher than 8mm.

## The Camera

Naturally, the decision you make about film size has a lot to do with your choice of camera—to an extent. Truthfully, both choices are interrelated. A feature of one may determine the selection of the other—and visa versa. But once you decide on size, the exact choice of camera will be based on individual characteristics that either appeal to you or that you need.

Let's not get any more involved in price than necessary at this point. Suffice to say, the more elaborate the camera, the more you can expect to pay. It's quite possible to buy a good used camera for as little as $25 or $30—or a new one for as much as a few thousand dollars.

Instead, let's consider the essential characteristics of the camera itself—size, film capacity, film load, viewfinder, lenses, and finally, features that are nice but not precisely necessary.

Film load: Whether you settle on 8 or 16mm, you'll have to decide between magazine and roll. There are advantages and disadvantages to both—and you'll have to balance them out against your own particular needs.

Roll film is definitely cheaper than magazine film. However, a magazine need only be slipped into the camera and you're ready to shoot. But, and this is a big one, image sharpness is better with roll film. And roll film cameras, even in 8mm models, offer greater motion picture flexibility. Finally, maximum total shooting footage of magazine film is 50 ft. Roll film loads on daylight spools hold as much as 200 ft.—although 100 ft. is the most common capacity for 16mm cameras and 25 ft. of double-8 (actually 50 ft.) for 8mm cameras.

## Lens Equipment

The lens is one of the most critical parts of a camera. Generally, lenses can be classed as focusing and fixed focus. Under most conditions, the focusing lens can be expected to provide sharper images—and the greatest amount of

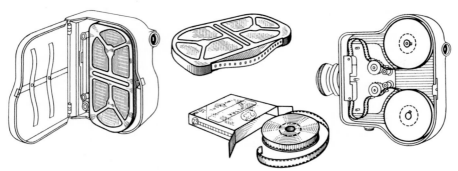

MAGAZINE-LOAD CAMERA. — Its operation is extremely simple because the film is contained in a magazine. Just placing the magazine inside loads the camera. Especially convenient where speed of handling is necessary

ROLL FILM CAMERA. — Only a bit more involved when loading than the magazine-load camera, but film is less expensive. The film can be wound backwards for dissolves, superimpositions and other special effects.

movie making flexibility. While most motion picture cameras don't have precise focusing mechanisms built into them—as do still cameras—it takes only a bit of practice to learn to use the depth of field scale, a ruler, or the hyperfocal distance of a lens for accurate focusing. While the manual that comes with every new camera has detailed focusing instructions, we'll go into focusing later on in this book.

You'll also have to decide whether you want a single lens camera, or one with a turret that accommodates two or three lenses. The normal lens, 25mm (1 in.) on 16mm cameras, 12½ or 13mm (½ in.) on 8mm cameras, covers an angle of view roughly equal to that of the human eye. But it cannot do the same job that the human eye can. The eye covers a lot of territory, linking together details in an almost unconscious way to give the brain a general impression of the scene in front of it. The human eye can isolate, fixing on a single detail, studying it carefully. The lens falls far short of what the eye can do.

Thus, several lenses—wide-angle, normal, and telephoto—are combined to provide something of the seeing power of the human eye. The tele provides a closer look at things for detail—while the wide-angle makes it possible to cover a wide expanse.

If your camera is equipped with three lenses you can handle most movie making situations quickly. Many single lens cameras provide for interchangeability of lenses—but unthreading one and replacing it with another takes time. A two or three lens turret makes for quick lens changing—almost less time than it takes to think about it.

Of course, the zoom-type lenses combine wide-angle normal, and telephoto in one lens. A variable element changes the focal length of the lens and at the same time makes possible some pretty useful optical effects.

Frankly, I'm pretty much in favor of a multiple lens system. It'll help you make better films—no matter what kind of motion pictures you decide to try your hand at.

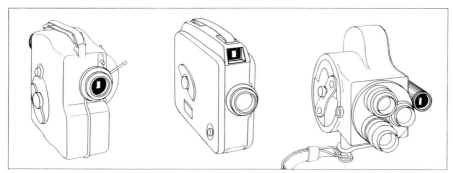

VIEWFINDERS. — The reflex viewfinder (left) directs the picture seen by the lens to your eye with a set of mirrors. With such a finder, the picture you see is always the picture the lens sees. The separate viewfinder (center and right) is placed either on top or on the side of the lens. There is, in this case, a parallax error which is negligible for long shots but which must be corrected for close-ups. (See drawing at the bottom of the page.)

## The Viewfinder

Obviously, anything as important as a device that shows you the exact framing of a scene is an essential piece of equipment. The most precise viewfinder is the reflex, or through-the-lens type. By a system of prisms and mirrors, it shows you the field just as the lens sees it. On some cameras, the Kodak Cine Special for example, you can view through the lens only when the camera is not in operation. Others, such as the Arriflex or the Bolex H-16 Reflex, show a continuous image even while shooting.

Make sure that your camera viewfinder, if it is separate from the lens system itself, presents the same field that the lens covers. Also, it should be flexible enough to cover a wide range of lenses. Make sure, too, that it is parallax corrected—not just for medium shots, but for extreme close-ups as well. Most cameras have some optical or mechanical device for parallax correction.

## Special Features

Actually, many of the things that we used to call "special" are rather common

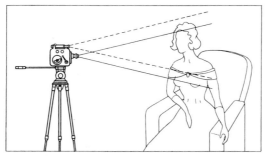

PARALLAX ERROR. — For any close-up shot framed with a separate viewfinder parallax error must be corrected. Here the finder frames the subject correctly but the lens cuts off the top of her head. This is a vertical parallax error. A special device on the viewfinder makes it possible to correct this.

on many cameras today. Let's look at some of these features. First, the not so special ones that you should expect on any camera anywhere in the neighborhood of $100—providing, of course, you don't invade the electric eye field.

Multiple film speeds: Normal silent speed is 16 fps, although a shift is being made toward 18 fps. Sound speed for films using an optical sound track, is 24 fps. However, magnetic sound striping may be used at either 16 or 24 fps. In addition, cameras are often equipped with 8, 12, 32, 48 and 64 fps speeds which allow a wide range of special effects and exposure control.

Single frame: The ability to expose only one frame at a time is the basis for animation and time lapse filming.

Variable shutter: A variable shutter serves two purposes, in that it allows exposure control by changing the exposure time at any fps speed (for example, by closing the shutter half way, you can half the exposure time at 24 fps. Instead of $\frac{1}{50}$ sec. you can shoot at $\frac{1}{100}$ sec.) Also, a variable shutter makes it easy to add fades and dissolves to your films right in the camera.

Backwind: Usually, the backwind is a small hand crank that permits winding exposed footage back on the feed spool. It can be used for special double exposure effects or to make a lap dissolve in conjunction with a variable shutter.

Frame counter: Not too many amateur cameras have them, but a frame counter is a mighty useful control for making dissolves or for animation and time lapse shooting.

Built-in Exposure Meter: There are roughly three types of exposure meters that couple to a movie camera. Some merely sit on top of the camera in an accessory shoe and perform in the same way as an ordinary exposure meter—with perhaps a bit less accuracy. A second type is actually built into the camera, and couples to the lens diaphragm for the correct exposure. A third type does all the work. It is connected to the lens diaphragm via an electrical circuit or mechanical hookup. In most 8mm cameras energy for the circuit comes from the light hitting the meter cell. The light is converted to energy and sets the diaphragm. However, electric eye systems are battery operated on 16mm cameras.

As you make films you'll think of any number of things you'd like to have on a camera. If you take a whirl at candid movie making you'll probably want some kind of viewer that will let you look in one direction while actually shooting in another. You may get thoroughly disgusted with spring wound cameras and latch on to a synchronous (24 fps only) or variable speed electric motor. Or you may need a grip or gunstock for specialized filming. But it's not the gadgets that make the films—its you.

## Film Choice—Black-and-White or Color

Let's take for granted that you've purchased your camera and projector and suddenly you broach upon the matter of choosing a film emulsion. Once you start looking around in magazines and on dealer shelves you'll realize that there's more than one film and certainly more than one company making raw film stock available. You're confronted with a confusing bunch of charts that give film speeds, color sensitivity, and a few dozen other assorted (or badly sorted) facts. The immediate attraction is color film—and in the last few years

American film manufacturers have expanded the list of color film considerably. Many so-called amateur films are used by professionals—and visa versa. Both 8 and 16mm color films are made in reversal stock only—that is film that shows a positive image after full development. While prints can be made quite successfully from a reversal original, when more than 25 are required professionals usually have an internegative made.

Color films are fairly easy to use but require somewhat more care than black-and-white. There are a few problems with color film that aren't encountered when using black-and-white films—exposure, editing, color rendition, among others. It might be a good idea if you haven't done much still or motion picture shooting to start your film making with black-and-white. Cost differences between black-and-white and color aren't really significant. However, black-and-white film stock may prove slightly less expensive. And since economics enter into film making it might be wise to check with your local film supplier on actual prices.

A wide range of black-and-white emulsions are available. Most of them are panchromatic—sensitive to all colors in terms of the gray scale. The difference is in the speed of each type of film.

Speed is usually expressed in a number based on the American Standards Association system for rating film. The number usually includes a safety factor. A slow film might have a rating of 40 and a fast one 200. Both often can be shot at faster or slower ratings, depending on lighting conditions, processing, and the effect you are after. Slow films are used either outdoors in sunlight or indoors with floods. A fast film may be used indoors with supplementary lighting or with just the available light.

Color films also come in various speeds—ranging from ASA 10 to 100. Color rendition may be slightly different with each type of film—and you'll have to learn a bit about that if you want to use color to its maximum advantage. There's really only one way—by experimenting with the available films. We'll go more thoroughly into the questions arising from black-and-white and color films later on in this book.

CHAPTER 3

# You Are the Script Writer

Why bother with script writing? For many film makers the answer is simple and direct—don't worry about scripts. These are the film makers who confine their shooting to record making—faces, slices of life, scenery, or some other incident that requires only a few feet of film. As long as the footage is well exposed, sharp, and easily identifiable you can live nicely without a script. But you just may want to go yourself one better.

Let's pose a situation that involves some of the color slides you may have shot last summer. After dinner or perhaps at a gathering of some kind, you decide to show your slides. Think about how you usually show them. You make at least some attempt to project them in sequence, linking the ones that deal in similar subjects. While the slides are on the screen you make comments on the time, place, and people. You may have even taken some of the slides that duplicate others out of the box—so as not to show them by mistake. All this adds up to editing—so that you have a rather interesting presentation instead of a draggy, boring one.

Films require even more of the same. It takes only a little film making to realize that scenes have a life of their own. And it is not only a mechanical one—but that each shot shows a definite tendency to unite with another, to complement other shots. Scenes that don't unite or complement other scenes are static, almost useless. Some scenes may be duplicates of others, presenting nothing new in the way of images or ideas and after a really terrific scene you have a blank which you can't fill. Other shots exhibit a too drastic change of angle—or no change at all. A man may walk into a scene and just walk out—and instead of panning with him, the camera remained stationary. Thus, we have a poorly planned film—and regrets. A little script *planning*, if not writing, might have avoided all that. Instead of shooting each scene in a filmic vacuum, a script would have provided you with an overall look at the whole film. Basically, all films tell a story and a successful story must have some kind of form, some planning.

## Still Photography and Motion Pictures

If there is a danger in transmitting still photo techniques to motion pictures it lies in not understanding the basic differences between the two mediums. People react in different ways to movies and to still pictures. A still photograph captures a moment in time and space—and here lies its strength. It almost forces you to reconstruct what happened before that moment, what can follow it, and to some extent what's around it. The still photograph makes your imagination work. How successful it is depends on how much it provokes your thinking.

But, on the other hand, a motion picture reconstructs life right before your eyes. It captures your attention and does not permit your imagination to work in the same sense that a still picture forces it to work. Life is there, in front of you, and you sit in front of the screen in much the same way that you might look out a window, or watch the action in a room. To be sure, the story must have some semblance of believability and facts must follow each other logically. It doesn't matter whether the film is a professional or amateur one. The series of images will have their own rhythm and speed. Gestures and facial expressions which you might like to see for longer periods of time vanish quickly—as they do in life.

The legitimate stage is in somewhat the same position as the still photograph. The stage is usually a bare impression of reality. The audience builds its own images around the framework of painted backdrop, a few sticks of furniture, and a semblance of walls. If the set is successful the image arises in the mind of the viewers. If it is not, the sticks remain sticks and the paint remains paint.

Thus, the film maker has a rather unique task—quite different from the still photographer or the stage director. He has to present consecutive images in a combination that takes on the full meaning of reailty and of presence—a sense of here and now.

The still photograph is stationary, almost static without imagination. The film must combine images into a moving, living, meaningful whole.


## Scene Composition

While you don't have to write a script—except for the film that deals with fiction or ideas—you must achieve through your camera the same logical order that you follow when showing slides. This should be borne in mind even for very short scenes that are perhaps complete in themselves. Your job as a film maker is to communicate with your audience. Clear, direct language is almost always the best way to present an idea.

Most amateur films are based on material gathered almost at random— short pieces of life recorded one after the other. One approach to scripting is to divide even a minor episode into the different elements that make it up— the background, people, and the action. Defining these elements presents what you have to say clearly.

Make it a point in your early film making to describe the background with several wide angle shots. Close-ups are best when describing people. Don't hesitate to use extreme close-ups if they'll best show a particular important movement. Let the audience see the action from several angles. Each movement in a total action has its very own best angle.

Suppose we decide to do a short film on a family outing to the country? Let's see if we can figure out the best way to do the story—and at the same time start channelizing our thinking into cinematic terms.

We shoot a few feet of film as the car travels through the neat looking countryside, getting images of red barns, shadowy roads, and rolling hills. The car reaches the picnic site. We use the same technique described in the first chapter. The driver turns the car around—after you get out with your camera—and drives back toward you. You follow the car as it moves to the spot where it will stop, cut to a long shot of the surrounding country and then move in close for some footage of everyone getting out of the car, unloading all the picnic gear, and preparing for the outdoor lunch. You shoot the willing but perhaps clumsy efforts of the youngsters, pan to a close-up of the main dish going from hand to hand. You dissolve or fade-out the shot and dissolve or fade-in the empty plate to provide a sense of time passing and things getting done.

Someone goes fishing, another rests under a tree or goes to sleep, the kids go swimming, and someone else inevitably gets stuck with cleaning up. You shoot it all. Shooting this way is much like editing right in the camera in the style of the Italian neorealists who made such films as Bicycle Thief and Open City. But this way is much more difficult than the conventional scripting method. The cameraman must have a certain amount of virtuosity—an ability that comes only with practice. But from the above, you can see that a good film is based on logical development—with things coming in order to tell an understandable story.

### The Shooting Script

Let's take a look at the way a professional film is written. Many of the scripting techniques of the pro are easily applied to amateur film making.

Naturally, someone has to come up with an idea. Usually, he presents the idea in synopsis form. This is followed by a film *treatment*—a fairly complete series of episodes which will make up the film. The final phase in the cycle is the shooting script—the last written form before the story goes before the cameras. It contains dialogue or the outline of the narration, and often, the way each shot will be made—angle, lighting, composition. But that depends on the particular director and how he likes to work.

Here, for example, is part of the shooting script for the French film "The Little World of Don Camillo." * The scene is the procession which has been boycotted by the civil servants and by the friends of Mayor Peppone.

#### The Church Square—Daylight

The Church Square, deserted. In the background, the church. Don Camillo comes in the doorway carrying a cross. He walks across the square singing a hymn.

#### Closer shot of Camillo—Dolly shot

The camera backs up in front of Camillo who walks, singing away as though

* Published with the permission of M. Julien Duvivier, director, and Rene Barjavel, screenwriter, of the film.

THE LITTLE WORLD OF DON CAMILLO, Julien Duvivier (1952). — Just by taking a look at the portion of the script reproduced here you can see that this shot of French actor Fernandel follows the script exactly. The scene is truly the concrete expression of the situation invented by the writer and composed by the director on paper.

(Photo by Cinedis)

nothing strange was going on. A dog comes along and starts to follow him. Don Camillo, still singing, tries to shoo him away with his foot. The dog stays. Don Camillo stops singing in order to address the dog.

### CAMILLO

—Go away!
He starts to sing again, not able to find the right key for a while. Same thing happens again. Finally Jesus starts to speak.
*Extreme close up of Christ on the Cross. Follow shot as the camera pans down to a close-up of Camillo*

### VOICE OF JESUS

—Leave him alone. This way Peppone won't be able to say there wasn't even a dog at the procession.

*Horizontal pan of the houses around the square*

One can guess that behind the closed shutters and the venetian blinds are hidden expectant faces, inquiring eyes.

*Dissolve to the street which leads to the river, shot from the top in a vertical angle*

The street is deserted; in the background, one can see the river and in front of it a line of people composed of Peppone and several hundred citizens wearing red ties blocking the street. Camillo enters the field from the back, in the bottom of the frame, followed by the dog.

*Pan to Camillo*

He sees the mass of people in his way.

*Pan to the young militants*

Their attitude is stern, immobile.

*Camillo appears in the foreground—Dolly shot*

He stops singing but keeps on walking. His face is furious and congested.

*Pan to Peppone who appears in the foreground*

He stands firmly, his legs apart and his arms folded.

*Dolly shot of Camillo*

He lifts the cross, waves it on top of his head and marches forward like a tank.

CAMILLO

—Be careful, Lord, hold on . . . I'm going to attack.
*Closer shot—Camera follows Camillo—The militants are standing in front of him*
The cross, in the foreground, advances toward the line of the demonstrators.

*Close-up of Camillo—Close-up of the Militants*
*Dolly shot (as before)*
The cross goes forward. Suddenly the militants appear undecided, then they open the way in the center of the street. Only Peppone stands firmly in the middle of the street.

*Wide-Angle Shot*

Camillo arrives next to Peppone and stops a second. They stare at each other, then Peppone points at the cross.

PEPPONE

—I don't back up because of you, but because of Him.

CAMILLO

—Take off your hat, then.

A SIMPLE COUNTRY TALE. — It's easier to imagine at the time of the script writing than to capture it with the camera. When the script calls for characters as unpredictable and as obstinate as a flock of sheep, it is obvious that the director may have to change his plans. *(Photo by Georges Régnier)*

For some directors the shot breakdown is just a flexible canvas on which only the dialogue appears in precise form; for others, on the other hand, this operation is extremely precise and the slightest detail is recorded in advance. In front of each number, each of which represents a shot (that is, a different angle of the camera). There are notes indicating the exact nature of each angle: extreme long shot, long shot, medium shot, medium close-up, close-up, extreme close-up, vertical shot and so on. (We shall see later on what is the exact meaning of these terms). Movements of the camera are also indicated if necessary (pan, dolly shot) as well as effects (dissolves, fades and special effects). In another column we find a description of the action, with details of the characters, their movements, the background and the props which will be used. Finally, in still another column, are the indications on sound; that is the dialogue, music, sound effects.

Here, as another example, is a portion—chosen because it is full of action—from the shot breakdown of a short film narration: "A Simple Country Tale."

### Shot Breakdown is Necessary

Some movie makers, who are in favor of a very thorough breakdown, go so far as to say that "a film is already made" when it is put down on a shooting script. Perhaps what they really mean is that a good film is written down before it can be shot, and that the difficulties that will be encountered later will be

## EXAMPLE OF SHOT BREAKDOWN

| Scene No. | Technical details—Action | Narration—Sound effects |
|---|---|---|
| 17 | *Long Shot*<br>The dog gathers the flock.<br>The flock starts moving.<br>(timing: approx. 10 sec.) | Sheep dog is a hard worker. It's time to go home, but first the sheep must get water. |
| 18 | Dissolve to medium long shot | |
| | (in the foreground, the pond) The impatient sheep come to the water to drink. The dog keeps a close eye on the flock.<br>(timing: 15 sec.) | Sound of the flock.<br>Bleating of the sheep.<br>Noise of the drinking animals. |
| 19 | *Close-up* (detail)<br>The sheep dip their noses in the pond water and draw the water in<br>(timing: 5 sec.) | |
| 20 | *Extreme close-up*<br>The dog is nervous, looks at something in the distance.<br>(timing: 4 sec.) | The dog growls. |
| 21 | *Extreme close-up*<br>The shepherdess, surprised, looks around. | |

| Scene No. | Technical details—Action<br>(timing: 5 sec.) | Narration—Sound Effects |
|---|---|---|
| 22 | *Extreme long shot*<br>Coming down from the hill a large flock is marching in a cloud of dust.<br>(timing: 12 sec.) | Bleating, tinkling of the large flock, sound of their hooves. |
| 23 | Again extreme close-up of the dog | |
| | (Same as Sc. 20)<br>The dog shows his teeth.<br>(timing: 3 sec.) | The dog growls. |

| | | |
|---|---|---|
| 24 | *Close-up*<br>The sheep, disturbed, lift their heads.<br>(timing: 5 sec.) | |
| 25 | *Long Shot—Pan*<br>The young shepherd is seen emerging from the flock of sheep. The sheep run toward the water.<br>(timing: 10 sec.) | Common usage requires that one flock go to drink only after another is finished, in order to avoid the sheep getting mixed. But this shepherd doesn't seem to care. |

| Scene No. | Technical details—Action | Narration—Sound Effects |
|---|---|---|
| 26 | *Extreme close-up again of the shepherdess* (same as Sc. 21)<br>She seems surprised and angry as she looks toward the shepherd.<br>(timing: 4 sec.) | Who is that? He usually doesn't take his sheep here. |
| 27 | *Close-up—Pan*<br>The shepherd throws his jacket over his shoulder and looks at her.<br>(timing: 5 sec.) | The girl recognizes him. He is a shepherd from the next village, a young man more fierce looking than his dogs. |

only technical ones. The scripts of Rene Claire, for example, are famous for their precision and detail.

Should the amateur movie-maker get involved in this kind of complicated business? Not for footage of a special occasion or a trip. Yes, if you tackle any kind of a more involved film: a documentary, or the telling of a story, or the projecting of an idea.

A while ago, in the section on the documentary, I suggested that you depict the life, during one day, of the place where you spend your vacation. A film of this kind, which depends primarily on spontaneous impressions, of images gathered here and there and edited together, can be made without written preparation. However, the results will be altogether more unified and harmonious if you think out the film in advance, allowing enough leeway for unexpected material.

Let's try to compose a portion of the breakdown of this film which exists thus far only in your imagination. For instance, the sequence about nightfall. (Narration would not be necessary for this film, as it would probably do nothing but repeat the image. Better to use a few sound effects and appropriate music.)

VILLAGE LIFE. — This scene could have been taken from our imaginary film. A medium long shot, large enough to give a feeling of space, frames the cart, nicely. The angle from beneath fully utilizes the sky. *(Photo by H. Albertus)*

| | | |
|---|---|---|
| *Long shot* (the sun is already low in the sky. Evening) | On one of the roads which leads to the village, a cart, heavily loaded with hay. | Calm music |
| *Pan* | The camera follows the cart which fills the screen. | |
| *Close-up* (detail) Camera slightly tilted upwards | Some children are seated on top of the cart in the hay. | |
| Extreme long shot | The square in front of the church. The shadows of the houses are lengthening. The minister walks across the square, enters the church. The steeple of the church with swallows flying around it. *(This shot could be used as a leitmotiv to indicate the passing hours of the day.)* | |

| | | |
|---|---|---|
| *Medium shot* | A woman takes out a chair and sits down in front of her door. | |
| *Long shot* (matching action) | Her neighbor does the same thing. They begin to chat. | |
| *Medium long shot* (against the light) | A young girl is walking a herd of cows back to the village. The sun goes down. | Fade in music |
| *Medium shot—Pan* | A housewife goes to the fountain with a couple of buckets. | |
| *Long shot*, slightly downwards. | The fountain. The woman enters the frame. Other women are around it already. | Sound of the running water and of the water falling into the bucket. Sound of the water will emphasize the meaning of the pictures throughout these scenes |
| *Close-up* | While she fills her buckets a woman talks. Another answers her. | |
| *Extreme close-ups* (to be alternated when editing) | A woman chatting. Another one. The running water. A third woman. The water. A full bucket. It overflows. | |
| *Long shot* (slightly downwards). | The yard of a farm. Buildings silhouetted against the light. A man has unharnessed his horses and takes them to the horse trough. | Music again. |
| Close-up (downwards) | Feet being wiped before entering a door | Same theme, but slower. |
| *Medium shot* (match action) | The man enters the farm | |
| *Medium close-up* (short pan) | Woman milking a cow. | |
| *Medium shot*, pan against the light. Light comes from the side on the edge of the wall | A child goes to buy some milk. He carries the bottle in one hand and jumps on one foot. | |
| *Wide angle* (upwards) | Silhouette of the church steeple against a clear sky. | The bell rings the hour. |

In the process of creating a script for a motion picture the movie maker must look squarely at his material. Instead of thinking in words he must think in terms of images, building a concrete picture in his mind. Despite all efforts, there will be gaps to fill in between what the film maker visualizes his film to be and the actual concrete shot specifications. Here's where the personality and individual talent of the amateur comes into play. But imagination and quality will have an easier time if the film's outline has been worked out as clearly as possible.

A shot or scene breakdown imposes discipline since it acts as a guide and reference source for the film's continuity. The shooting script stands between you and the temptation to go far afield, chasing some particular element in the film that appeals to you. The danger there, of course, is overdevelopment of one aspect of the film in detriment to the others.

Occasionally, the temptation to create a previously unplanned scene just because the various elements required were available has led me right into trouble. Almost every time, the error showed up at the editing bench. Even when the scene was really beautiful and had its own interest values—it didn't fit in with the rest of the footage. It destroyed the rhythm of the film and eventually it was discarded.

Don't think for a moment that a script will enervate a film—killing off its vitality. Almost any motion picture has a basic strength that protects it. You need to impose limitations if you are to project the idea to an audience.

Before we lay aside the matter of scripts—for now at least—I'd like to make a comment on the Italian neorealist school of film making. Actually, much that I have said may seem opposed to the Italian school. In reality, it is not.

In the neorealistic type of film we are immediately attracted to the natural aspects of life—the vivacity, spontaneity, absence of artificiality. The sum total of what we see is a feeling of an improvisation—a film shot almost as life occurs, without apparent plan or preconception.

One thing that the Italian director has to work with in making this kind of film a success is the character of the Italian people who never quite separate life from acting. They assume for themselves any of several parts—gay, comic, tragic.

But no matter how accidental films such as *La Strada, Open City,* or any number of other great Italian films seem to be, a lot of planning went into each one. Perhaps the margin of freedom between script and film is somewhat greater than ordinarily encountered in film making. Certainly the emphasis is on human values and not on technical perfection. But, these films were planned. Cameramen, director and actors just didn't go out into a street in Naples and start making a movie from scratch. So, there really is no conflict between what I have said and the Italian school.

One conclusion sounds almost like a paradox—the more you are able to work out an idea on paper, the freer you'll make your camera for instilling greater expressiveness into a film. The experience you acquire in planning spills over to the films where planning isn't really needed—family type movies, for example.

Basic, of course, to experience is the ability to use the tools of film making—particularly the camera. Once you know your camera well, you can make it do what you want. So, let's talk about camera work, before we embark on the role of the director.

# CHAPTER 4

# You Are the Cameraman

If you've done any still shooting at all a little additional shooting with a movie camera should prove to you that getting the right exposure is no more involved with one than with the other. Technical requirements for adequate exposure are the same for both. Boiled down to its simplest form this is the problem—to get enough light through the lens to record an image on a sensitive surface. We regulate the amount of light in two ways—by controlling the shutter speed or the lens diaphragm opening. But let's take a quick look—a sort of refresher—at the technical aspects of exposure, because adequate exposure, along with image sharpness and camera steadiness will determine the technical quality of your film.

## Exposure

Actually, the matter of one of the variables of exposure, the shutter speed, is pretty well decided for us. Normally, we shoot at 16 fps for silent films and 24 fps for sound. The fps rate, of course, determines the shutter speed. The movie shutter is actually a circular disc, with a portion cut out. When this cut out portion is in front of the lens aperture light passes through the lens to the sensitive emulsion. When the film moves, the opaque portion of the shutter swings in front of the film, cutting off the light. The circular action of the shutter is powered by the electric or spring wind motor of the camera.

At 16 fps, exposure ranges from $\frac{1}{30}$ to $\frac{1}{40}$ sec., depending on the camera. At 24 fps, the speed is normally $\frac{1}{50}$ sec. A variable shutter, discussed in a previous chapter on equipment, makes it possible to make the cut out section of the shutter smaller, thus decreasing the exposure time. But unless you have a variable shutter, you have a choice of only one shutter speed per fps rate.

Of course, shooting at 8 or 32 or some other fps speed entails a different shutter speed, and upon occasion serves as an exposure control. But those additional speeds on your camera are almost strictly for special effects.

Actually, since you'll do most of your shooting at normal speeds in order to present a natural appearing image, the only real control you have over exposure is the lens diaphragm.

## The Lens Diaphragm

Let's assume you never saw a lens before. Just what do those numbers mean— f/1.4, f/1.9, f/2.5, f/4, f/5.6, f/8 and f/16? Well, f/1.4 represents the largest opening of the lens. At this diaphragm opening the lens admits the most light. Each succeeding number halves the amount of light. For example, at f/8 you're allowing only half the light to hit the film than you did at f/5.6. At f/11 only half the light admitted at f/8 reaches the film, and so on. The largest number on any lens admits the least light—the smallest number the most light. Speed of a lens is usually expressed in the greatest amount of light it will admit.

Your camera lens is an imitation of nature—much like the pupil of a human eye which opens and closes according to the amount of light it encounters. The diaphragm is like the iris of your eye, consisting of leaves that open and close as you rotate a control wheel on the lens. The precise opening you use depends on the amount of light on the subject, the speed of the film, and perhaps the effect you want.

At one time the diaphragm opening was a matter of experience combined with a calculated guess. Today, exposure meters do most of the work.

## The Exposure Meter

The exposure meter is a "must have" piece of equipment. It's a good idea to hang it from your neck with a chain or similar carrying system—for two reasons. You'll always have it handy and it won't be in danger of sudden tragic accidents—such as hitting rocks, pavements, floors or other hard, unyielding objects.

Practically any exposure meter designed for still cameras can be used for motion pictures. Some of the newer ones even have fps indications, 16, 24, 32, 48 and 64. However, there are some meters designed only for movie work.

Exposure meters fall into two general categories—incident and reflected light. A reflected light meter measures the light reflected by a subject. An incident light meter measures the light hitting the subject. There are arguments for both types. However, the reflected light meter is in greater use—particularly for still photography. Many professionals prefer the incident light type—specially for shooting with artificial light indoors. It provides an overall reading for the set more readily than the reflected meter. A reflected meter requires taking several readings for the various light levels and then averaging them all. The incident light meter is used from the camera position, giving an overall reading for all the light hitting the subject. However, the reflected light meters tend to be more sensitive to low light in many cases. Also, incident light readings under many circumstances require the addition of experience to achieve the correct f-number.

But, both meters, used properly, are invaluable to the motion picture maker.

## Focusing and Depth of Field

Practically speaking, the focusing problem for motion pictures is considerably less than for still pictures. Compared to lenses used for 35mm still photography, optics for movies are of shorter focal length. Where a 50mm lens is the standard for 35mm still cameras, the normal lens for a 16mm camera is 25mm or one inch, while 12½ or 13mm is normal for 8mm. The smaller the lens opening and the shorter the focal length the greater the depth of field at a

DIAPHRAGM. — The correct exposure depends on the diaphragm, which allows more or less light to hit the film.

A. — Too much of an opening for a given amount of light *overexposes* the image, and washes out shadows. This type of scene lends itself to overexposure—very bright sky, white houses and white boat, sun-drenched dock.

B. — A *correctly exposed* scene reproduces the subject over a full tonal range and that includes pure whites and pure blacks. When measuring the light with the meter, it is necessary to carefully avoid the strong reflected light from the houses, the ground and the light foreground.

C. — Too small an opening of the lens *underexposes* the scene giving an impression of night. Here the whites were so strong that they managed to come through, and the scene is not in itself unpleasant. But it obviously gives a wrong impression. It fails to convey the atmosphere of the small harbor drenched in midday light.
(*Photos by Jacques Boulas*)

given distance. A 25mm lens has a greater depth of field (or zone of sharp focus) at a given distance and diaphragm opening than a 50mm lens. This depth of field, or zone of sharp focus as it's sometimes called, is the near and far distance that objects are in apparently sharp focus.

Many lenses have a depth of field scale engraved on the lens barrel. The scale shows the exact distance from in front of the camera lens to beyond the subject that you are in focus at a particular footage setting.

Most focusing movie lenses must be set by hand. That is, you either measure or approximate the distance and set the footage scale. Of course, if you have a reflex through-the-lens focusing camera, you can focus precisely on the camera ground glass.

Since the shutter speed is fixed, and the lighting conditions determine how small or large the diaphragm opening should be, you really can't always depend on selecting a small opening to give you maximum overall sharpness.

In bright sunlight, however, using even slow color film, your opening will be at least f/8 to f/11. In bad light, the problem is more difficult because you may have to shoot wide open to obtain adequate exposure. Thus, you'll have to determine what is important enough in the scene to be sharp and select a footage setting that will give you a depth of field that will encompass those elements.

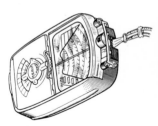

LIGHT AND SHADOW. — A scene like this one, which was shot under the beautiful Oudaias Gates in the ancient portion of Rabat, in Morocco, presents some difficult problems. It is composed equally of dark shade and of bright light. The exposure meter gives you different readings according to whether it is aimed at one side or the other. The truth in this case lies between an average reading, although it should be closer to the highlight reading as the eye is attracted more toward the brighter portion of the picture. The shadows are slightly sacrificed and will appear primarily as a frame.
(Photo by Georges Régnier)

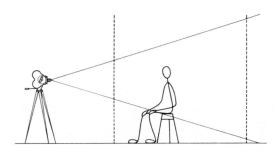

**DEPTH OF FIELD.** — The expression "depth of field" refers to the area which appears sharp in front and in back of the subject on which the lens is focused. The area varies at a given distance between camera and subject according to the lens used (a wide angle lens gives a greater depth of field than a normal lens at the same F-number and distance), and the diaphragm opening (the smaller the diaphragm, the greater the depth of field).

Incidentally, depth of field decreases as subject and camera draw nearer to each other. Best way to determine focus setting, if you can't focus directly through the lens is to use a tape measure. This system is an absolute must for accurate focusing for extreme close-ups.

The very fact that we deal with movement creates another focusing problem. As the main subject moves in and out of the focus range, it most naturally goes in and out of focus. This is what the professional who does not have a through-the-lens focusing camera does to meet the situation.

First, he determines the maximum, intermediate and minimum footage settings for the scene. Then, he marks them on the footage scale of the lens. An assistant, watching the action, gradually moves the footage scale to the correct position as the action takes place. This follow-focus technique helps to keep the image sharp at all times. Takes a little practice, but it's worth it.

Focusing is particularly important with telephoto lenses. Depth of field, compared to normal lenses used at the same distance and lens setting, is small. There's no restriction on the use of a tele lens despite what you may have heard. It can be used to isolate a near subject—as well as enlarging the image of a distant object.

But avoid panning with a tele from one subject to another. Focusing is extremely critical and even the slightest difference between the distance of two subjects can result in one image being soft. Shoot the two separately—or use follow-focus if you *must* pan.

To recap what we've said (and to elaborate a bit, too), depth of field is your main focusing tool. It can also be used to emphasize one subject over another, by making one sharper, and the other a bit softer. Incidentally, depth of field is usually greater beyond the main point of focus than in front of it.

### Lens Choice

I've already mentioned that one lens can be chosen over another to obtain an effect (a tele to isolate the main subject, for example), but there's a great deal more to it. In many cases, the lens you choose will be dictated by shooting conditions. You can't move back far enough to take in the whole shot with a normal lens so you use a wide-angle, or you can't get close enough for detail so you choose a tele. But lenses do other things than magnify or minify. You can achieve greater pictorial meaning through using them for special effects.

CHOICE OF THE LENS. — Lenses of different focal lengths have different angles of view and optical peculiarities which must be used carefully.

A. *Wide-angle lens.* — The lens here covers the building of the Museum of Modern Art in Paris in all its architectural composition. The picture is very sharp and somewhat static. Also, there is an apparent distortion of the vertical lines which is rather unpleasant. For a shot like this one, it would have been better to use a normal lens and to shoot from a greater distance.

B. *Normal Lens.* — The shot made exactly from the same position is much more satisfactory. It brings the various subjects back to their real distance. The lines do not deviate. However, the shot would be better with people in the foreground. A pan would overcome the smaller angle of view.

C. *Telephoto lens.* — This lens fills almost the entire frame with the piece of sculpture; however, foreground and background are compressed. There is no feeling of depth. Note the flatness of the lines of perspective. Oblique lines are practically horizontal.

(*Photos by Jacques Boulas*)

For example, the *apparent* perspective changes when you switch from a wide-angle to a telephoto lens. With the wide angle, things seem to have a great deal of space between them. While with a tele, objects in a scene appear squashed together. Actually, it's only an illusion. The perspective hasn't been changed and if a portion of the wide-angle shot were enlarged to match the dimensions of the tele shot, the perspective would look precisely alike. The change is only apparent—but useful. You may want to express the spaciousness of a room or someone's surroundings with a wide-angle, or show the close relationships of things at a beach with a tele, for example. Or, you can emphasize the importance of a single element in a scene by using a tele to make it sharp while other objects are out of focus.

## Use of Different Focal Lengths

We've already noted that the wide-angle provides airiness or spaciousness to a scene. It also makes movements toward the camera appear faster, makes near and far objects appear sharper at a given f-number and footage setting than a normal or tele lens, and creates a feeling of a third dimension or depth, to the image.

There's a certain amount of distortion with extreme wide-angle lenses— usually 10 to 17mm for 16mm cameras, 5 to 7.5mm for 8mm machines. Make sure that you hold the camera absolutely level to minimize distortion when shooting vertical planes. Distortion can be quite obvious when shooting from above or below with wide-angle lenses, too. Movement also emphasizes distortion. But distortion can also be put to work to create a new image (with 5.6mm lens for 16mm) or a new way of seeing things. A distorted view of a skyscraper in the heat of the day, may be much more forceful than a shot that shows it as it normally looks.

The normal lens, since it is the one most often used and associated with the way the human eye sees things, shows the image in normal perspective.

The tele, compared to the normal lens, isolates the subject and is the classic tool for the close-up. But no lens can be really defined. Only the viewfinder and your own imagination can tell you what a lens will do. You may see something that no one has ever discovered. You may find a combination of shots using all your lenses that is breathtaking—or, use a lens to shoot a subject from an angle no one ever investigated before you tried it.

## Camera Movement

Make it a hard, fast rule—the camera rests firmly on a tripod whenever possible. Break the rule only when it's justified and that means when it is the only possible way to get a shot. Most 8 and 16mm cameras are light and compact—an advantage that leads us into the paths of temptation. An image that jumps all over the screen is distracting—and this is just the result you can expect from indiscriminant camera movement. The movement of the subject is the only guide and justification to camera movement. Even professionals can be guilty of excessive camera movement.

Movement of the image is the key to good films. Occasionally, movement stems from the camera. Also, in motion pictures, there's another kind of movement too—scene to scene and shot to shot. Let's imagine a scene composed of

DOLLY SHOT FROM A CAR. — A platform on top of your car allows the placing of the camera for a dolly shot. However, the camera is liable to pick up the movements of the car so choose a smooth road and ask the driver to stay in second gear and to keep a steady speed.

*(Photo by Georges Régnier)*

a group of people. We can move the camera steadily from face to face. But better still we can cut from face to face to show the counterplay of emotions much more powerfully. Here we have a stationary camera, but intense movement supplied by good cutting technique. The tripod is the cornerstone of discipline. You have to think about it in order to take camera off the pan head, or to move the pan head itself. It places a mechanical device between you and impetuous camera handling. The tripod is an absolute must for telephoto shooting, for close-ups, for precise framing, and for maximum image steadiness.

## The Pan and the Dolly Shot

The one word in the lexicon of the movie maker that anyone—even someone only mildly interested in films—is bound to know is the word *pan*. Short for panorama, you probably know that it means to move the camera either vertically or horizontally (or both) to cover a scene. You can follow an action or show an entire landscape in one "take." A pan to be successful must be made smoothly and as slowly as possible. The best type of pan shot is made with a combination of two directions so that the lens makes a curved or diagonal track rather than a straight line.

And then there's the dolly shot. In a dolly shot the camera actually moves forward, to the side, or back in relation to the action.

PANNING. — The first purpose of a pan is a course to follow the movement of a mobile subject in front of the camera. However, the subject can be nothing but a pretext to shoot an interesting background.

A. We were thinking of taking a shot of this street in a small Spanish town, all bathed in sun, when these two priests happened to walk through it. They made an excellent addition to the background, and we followed them with a pan.

B. When they passed the camera we framed them perfectly. Very little leeway was left around them.

C. When two unsuspecting actors went past us we stopped the pan on a frame which showed the other end of the street. The movement of the camera would have been pretty much unjustified without the two priests. It made an excellent shot with human interest added to the picturesque background.

(*Photos by Jacques Boulas*)

THE ZOOM LENS. — Here is an indication of how the lens works. We start with a long shot (represented by the whole surface of the photograph) showing the scenery on which the skiers are to appear. We then zoom in to a closer shot which shows a few skiers (this tight or frame is indicated by the printed line). The motion forward of the lens combined with the approach of the skiers will make their speed seem even greater and the effect is spectacular. We then use a follow shot which will combine with the panning effect. *(Photo by Georges Régnier)*

Professional dollies are made either on a vehicle moving along tracks or on rubber tires for maximum smoothness. But you can make a dolly on almost anything that offers a degree of smooth travel—car, boat, sled, cart or just about any wheeled vehicle. The important thing to look for is a steady platform that provides motion without jar or bumps. Plans have been published in various magazines, (MODERN PHOTOGRAPHY in the United States) for home-made dollies. Power for movement comes from someone pushing the tripod-mounted camera on the platform, while the platform itself rides on rails. Avoid using anything that might add jerkiness to the movement—such as a tow rope.

But the dolly shot leaves a lot of room for the inventive cameraman. If you're a good skier, your skis may make an excellent dolly. You might even use them indoors on a smooth surface.

The zoom lens already mentioned makes it possible to imitate the dolly shot without ever moving the camera. They are available in both 8 and 16mm and are made by several manufacturers. The lever action changes the focal length to give the appearance of either moving toward or away from an object in one smooth motion. The lens offers the flexibility of three lenses and at the same time the advantages of special effects. You aim the camera at a crowd,

A DOLLY SHOT ON SKIS. — Of course not everybody can dolly this way. This difficulty apart, there is no doubt that a snow covered slope is the ideal ground for a smooth and steady dolly shot. It may be safer, though, to use a sled. (*Photos by Georges Régnier*)

move the lever for a tighter frame, continue the zoom to isolate one face, and all in one movement.

## Using the Pan and the Dolly

Your role as director has a lot to do with when and where you'll use a dolly or a pan shot. We've intimated that the logical movement of a subject is the controlling factor in camera movement. And the panning shot is the most immediate way to keep a mobile subject in the frame. For example, you might pan on a moving car, an airplane taking off, a racing skier, or a swimmer dashing into the surf.

The pan helps you to catch the unexpected—the spontaneous movement such as a child running after a bird, a cat playing with a moving shadow. When there are a number of actions the pan can follow one given subject—a baseball player during a game—or a single object—the ball.

The dolly shot is a more elaborate undertaking than the pan and a bit more difficult to do successfully. It also reproduces a feeling of moving—similar to watching a landscape from a moving train. But you can follow the action much longer with a dolly than with a pan. Since in the dolly shot the camera stays with the action all the way, the image can remain the same size on the screen. The camera may precede the action—such as when the camera is in a car and moves in front of the car being filmed. It may ride alongside the subject—as

PICTURES LINKED BY A PAN. — The panning shot can link together two aspects of one single action here, a potter and the vase he is working on. The movement of the camera is not only the "mechanical" device to switch from the close-up of the artisan to the object which is taking form in his hands—it has also a stronger meaning. The pan creates an invisible tie between the man and the object to which he is giving shape. It goes from the thought and the eye to the hand. We see here a form of expression which is truly characteristic of the motion picture.

*(Photo by Jacques Boulas)*

when it travels with a bicyclist. It may even follow the subject—moving behind two strollers, for example.

In addition, both the pan and the dolly can be employed to clarify or to emphasize the intentions of the film maker. Both can be used to link details in a scene—the discovery of a capital atop a column, for one thing. A dolly or

53

pan that moves from a climber to a view of the valley below establishes a proportion and relationship.

The pan can tie together two different aspects of one action—the face of the sculptor and the piece on which he is working.

What we have said about the uses of the pan apply equally to the dolly shot. The dolly, in any case, is usually tied in with a pan—making it a much more flexible instrument. It can pick out individuals in a crowd, bring one close to another, isolate a fleeting expression and then follow the object of the expression, or even take the place of a character on the screen in such a way that the audience identifies completely with the character. Because the possibilities for using the dolly and the pan are endless, they are together with editing, the means by which a film achieves a language of its own.

## Thinking Like a Cameraman

A cameraman has to be something more than a shutter release pusher or an exposure meter handler. Think about each shot you make from several angles. If you don't you may find that you inadvertantly lopped off a few heads in an important shot. It might be a good idea to keep a small margin of safety between the top of a character's head and the limits of the frame.

And remember, it also is your job to see that the images have continuity. Colors, if you shoot color film, should be well balanced, and match for the best effects. If you use black-and-white film, colors should be rendered fully in terms of the gray scale. But, remember, the film idea is more important than technical perfection. Don't squeeze the vitality from the film with excessive posing and preparation.

And now, let's get on to the director—and that's you, too. While we've sidestepped several technical questions, we haven't forgotten about them. We'll discuss them fully later in the chapters on interiors, exteriors and places to shoot.

CHAPTER 5

# You Are the Director

As a film maker your main role in the whole scheme of things is that of a director. When you think about a film, you probably think about it in directorial terms. You've conceived an idea for a film, written a scene-by-scene script, and now you've reached the production stage. You're about to enter an area of film making that you perhaps are unfamiliar with—to assume a job that is as much a matter of your personal conception and creation as it is one whose techniques must be learned.

If it's any consolation at all, the professional director suffers as many doubts as the amateur as he shoots his first scene. He faces the task of molding, according to his own ideas, highly complex artistic and technical elements. He has to weld lighting, story, composition, expression of feeling, and the dialogue into a unified whole. The people he works with are individuals, each with a particular temperament. He faces the problem of imposing his own views—exercising tact on one hand and a certain amount of stubbornness on the other. He carries the entire film on his shoulders—living and breathing with it almost to the film's peculiar rhythm. The director alone has the responsibility for the final success or failure of the movie.

But you aren't a professional—and for that very reason operating in a much freer atmosphere. This is something you do for fun—for your own enjoyment. You have a workable schedule and you aren't confounded by the necessity of working with a large crew or bulky equipment. Neither oversensitive actors or the compulsion to shoot 15 scenes in one day weigh you down. Well, you may have some of those problems—but to a much lesser degree. But one thing you do have in common with the professional director—the desire to produce a successful motion picture, particularly in the eyes of your severest critic, yourself.

I've mentioned that the job of the director is as much a matter of personal concept and creation as it is one whose techniques must be learned. What it adds up to is this:

*The director must know the rules of his trade and invent the rest.*

A great deal of the success of a director depends on his instincts and a combination of qualities. He must have a sense of living and life similar to that of the novelist or the newspaper reporter. He must also have a taste for composition of lines, masses and light—almost in the same way that a painter or sculptor has it. Even a latent musical talent might be helpful. We all have these "instincts" to a greater or lesser degree.

But along with these innate qualities there are things that can be acquired by practice. They are the rudiments of a technical grammar learned through experience or schooling.

## Scenes and Takes

Everyone starts out with one idea no matter if the film is a recording of personal events, a report, a travelogue or a fiction story. The main point is to make the film an interesting and pleasant experience for the audience. The best approach you can take is to adopt as many professional methods as practicable. And really, this is almost a necessity in view of your audience—because no matter who it is composed of, professional standards are the ones by which they will judge your film. So some of the traditional rules, even a few that your imagination rebels against, must be accepted.

Accepting the rules, the first step is to make a shot by shot breakdown of the script when the film permits it. Or else, if you have a neorealist bent, plan to work straight from life, to capture a spontaneous quality.

But no matter how you approach the planning of your film, it will be composed of a certain amount of shots. A number of these "takes" combine to make a scene. Of course, a scene can be composed of only one take photographed from only one angle. Or, it can be composed of several shots put together on the editing bench. A scene may be a filmic jig saw puzzle, cut into small pieces by the camera, and then spliced together by the editor.

The first movies were composed of a few scenes, or even one scene, shot entirely from the same angle. Today, even the simplest story is shot from many angles to explain the action. Obviously, we've come a long way from the static film making of the pioneer days. Today, a scene composed of several shots from various angles is more alive, more meaningful since it permits the audience to figuratively look at the same action through the eyes of several people.

In fact, the art of the motion picture can be summed up by saying that it offers the possibility of transporting the viewer to the best viewing position in relation to the action. Here lies the film's faculty for persuasion, flexibility in the art of story telling and the ability to grasp the viewer's attention.

There are many examples of how the film has learned to fully use the power for seeing. But let's look at one of the greatest, to see how really effective is this power—the Odessa staircase scene in Sergei Eisentstein's *Potemkin*. The great Russian director shot the scene in such a way that the spectator finds himself at every spot on the staircase, together with each of the characters who watch the inexorable advance of the soldiers shooting at regular intervals into the crowd. One is not caught up only with the emotions of the main characters, but of the entire mass of people. Time is lengthened and multiplied as each second of the tragedy is lived several times through the reactions of the various actors. Only motion pictures, in the hands of a great artist, can convey this feeling of an unforgettable tragedy.

ROWING. — Illustrated on the following pages is an example of a shot-by-shot breakdown. It might be called a "condensation" of a film. Look at these photographs in numerical order, jumping rapidly from one to the next. Look for a feeling of rapid movement.

**1.** The signal is about to be given for the race to begin. The picture is calm, composed horizontally.

**5.** The body in action, the strain of the muscles is apparent in this extreme close-up.

**2.** The race has started, both boats rush forward. The shot taken from above, gives a high angle view of the race.

**6.** The blade of an oar is about to hit the water. The shot follows the movement, catching the surge created as it comes out of the water.

**3.** One team is already slightly ahead of the other as action is filmed from one of the boats.

**7.** Close-up of one of the oarsmen. The expression of his face.

**4.** The coxswain gives the beat to the oarsmen. This is a close-up, tight on the action.

**8.** One team is far ahead of the other. Medium shot.

9. And then immediately a close-up on a rower.

13. The bow of the boat jumps on the surface of the water.

10. Another medium shot of the rowers. One oar in the foreground indicates the opposing team is coming back strongly.

14. The effort at the finish.

11. A close-up of the coxswain, his face tense.

15. The finish. Victory by one length. The long shot taken from above shows the exact position of both teams.

12. Another close-up of an oarsman.

16. The race is over. Everyone relaxes. The scene is calm again.　　　(Photos by Michel Cambazard)

## Molding a Scene

The scene from *Potemkin* described above is an example of multiple action with the idea of time temporarily stopped. Let's compare it with a scene you might produce—a rowing race perhaps consisting of two eight-oar shells on a river. The action, broken down, consists of the race itself, the uncertainty of the outcome, the efforts of the oarsman, and the reaction of the spectators along the river bank. To reproduce the intensity of the scene the camera has to be everywhere at once:

1. Boats on the river.
2. On the water next to competitors showing progress of both teams.
3. On the faces of the oarsmen to show concentration and effort.
4. On the coxswain to follow the rhythm of his beat.
5. On the blades as they cut the water.
6. On the progress of the race to show loss and gain as registered by reactions of fans.
7. Behind the binoculars of the judges.
8. Viewing the minutes tick away on the stop watches of the judges.
9. Showing the tensing of muscles.
10. Seeing faces grow strained with effort.
11. Watching the few feet of water separating the shells.
12. The thunderous reaction of the spectators at the finish.
13. The reaction of the winners and the losers.

We've broken down the race into the many facets which actually compose it. We film the race shot by shot according to the breakdown and later the entire scene will be reconstituted on the editing bench (we'll look at the race again in the chapter on editing, but you may want to see opposite page).

You would need several cameras to shoot the script simultaneously. You can't be everywhere at once, but planning makes it possible to cover all the angles you'll need in succession. You needn't worry about shooting the film in sequence, just as long as the working schedule is carefully established. Actually, it's quite possible to shoot the end of many films long before the beginning is photographed.

In our own film of the rowing race, it's obvious that the wide angle shots showing both shells, must be photographed at the beginning. These long shots may be the only ones shot during the actual race, since camera movement during the race may be difficult. Later, close-ups can be filmed to conform to the general race pattern. You may be able to arrange a follow shot from a motor boat for takes of the rowers, judges, spectators and other elements. You'll have to hold a tight rein, as director, on continuity.

Summing up what we've said, you'll have to choose strongly expressive elements in order to depict forcefully a particular action. These elements can be gestures, attitudes, intentions, or any meaningful movement. The scene is filmed a piece at a time and remolded during editing. Time itself is recomposed. Remember, cinema time differs from real time, in that you can lengthen or shorten it in accordance with the needs of your film.

## Time and Motion Pictures

There's a lot to be said about the relationship between time and motion pictures. Motion pictures, which have a time element connection in an art

sense, use actual time as a vehicle. On the other hand, actual time is controlled—expanded or shrunk to conform with cinema time. The constant inter-
play of time and of the moving image plays an important part in the construction of a film.

The motion picture has imposed on the audience—as well as upon its crea-
tors—the necessity for seeing images more quickly. In a recent talk on "The
Tyranny of Time in the Movies," the French film maker, Jean Renoir, stated
the movies have "invented a new form of story telling." There is necessary
change that has to be made between real time of an action and the way you
show it on a movie screen. In the Odessa scene, above, Eisenstein chose some
particularly dramatic moments of the action to tell the story on film. The story
is told through episodes linked with particular people. The character is shown
for a time, left for another shot and then shown again. At the same time,
Eisenstein introduces a rhythmic repetition of the shooting soldiers walking
down the stairs. Time seems to be multiplied by the details of specific actions
combined into one major action.

Time is also suspended, stopping just as it does for us every time we reach
a crucial point in our lives. The idea of time in this sense is both collective
and subjective. It is true to reality, because we know that one minute can
sometimes flash by quickly—or drag interminably. The director plays with time
according to the demand of his subject. He can, as in the rowing race, show
time in relation to several characters taking part in the same action at the same
time. Or he can treat time subjectively, showing it in relation to one individual
action.

We have shown time multiplied and now let's take a look at it being shortened. Let's take as an example of a subjective time value that appears too short
in time for the action that it expresses—a man catching a train.

Our character is a businessman on a trip. He wears an overcoat, carries an
attache case, and looks like all businessmen. He hails a cab, and tells the driver
"to Grand Central Station, and hurry."

He looks at his watch: 10:40 am. His train leaves at 10:57 and he has a
lot of traffic to get through. That 17 minutes can be shown in a series of short
images which won't take more than roughly 1½ minutes of screen time. Here's
one way it might be done:

1. An exasperating traffic jam.
2. His watch showing 10:48.
3. The red light that never seems to turn green.
4. The watch again. This time its 10:50.
5. A policeman halts traffic just as the cab reaches an intersection.
6. Gesture of helplessness by the cabbie.
7. Clock on the railroad station reading 10:55.
8. Businessman bolting out of cab.
9. Running down platform.
10. Jumping on the train as it starts to move.

Here we've constricted time. With well directed, imaginatively photographed
and well edited shots, the audience figuratively lives the entire 17 minutes in

a much shorter space of time. And since the actual 17 minutes seems much shorter to anyone actually involved in catching a train, the actual screen time will seem real.

## The Experimental Approach

The amateur has a tremendous amount of freedom to experiment. Unfortunately, if one is to use the films shown at various amateur competitions as examples, this freedom is rarely exercised to discover new approaches to making films. All too often, the amateur will take the easy way out. Rarely will he risk film stock and his own time in an attempt to produce a new way of saying or showing a cinematic situation.

The usual way of expressing time, for instance, is through the medium of a ticking clock or a verbal expression of the hour. A fade-out indicates the end of one scene and a fade-in the beginning of a new one. The optical effect is a means for telling the audience that time has passed.

But supposing for a moment we feel that a fade slows the pace of our film. Could a symbol take the place of the optical effect? Perhaps as simple a device as a perfectly still shot of bare trees, or a windy beach intercut between two scenes might do it. The ideas we've suggested intimate a timelessness. They also motivate the audience toward thinking of change.

And do time and place really have to be pinned down? No, they do not. In the English film "The Bespoke Overcoat," the director, cameraman, and actors are dealing with a story first written by a Tsarist Russian. The film itself tells the same story in modern dress—or almost modern dress. But time is never explicit. The story could have taken place, today, yesterday, last week, or even in the last century. In fact, the film involves itself with flashbacks so much that the past and the present become almost one.

But experimentalism of this type requires adequate planning. The lines of continuity must never be severed. In the "Bespoke Overcoat" the overcoat plays the dominant role—providing the important focal point for the audience. It makes possible almost complete acceptance of what might easily be termed unreality.

Time and place may be artistically changed in other ways. For example in a film called "Moment in Love," produced by Shirley Clarke, two dancers are shown against a background of ruined buildings. The scene cuts to a mountain, and then to a lake. There is no relation in the dance and its backgrounds to reality. In fact, the aim was to avoid reality so as to highlight the meaning of the film.

But you cannot indiscriminately switch time and place. There must be a reason. Here is where intuitive directing (and editing) plays an important part. If the cut and the treatment of the time sense works for you, then it may work for the audience. However, at best you are gambling. This, of course, is the major premise of experimental movie making. You are making a bet on your ability to project a completely subjective idea.

But experimenting just to be different is pointless. There must be reason and meaning in every motion picture image. The reasons and meaning may be strictly personal—but they must be present if you are to communicate to an audience.

## THE IMAGING OF THE PASSAGE OF TIME

**1.** 10:40 "Hey, taxi!"

**2.** "To the station, quick!"

**5.** "If we don't get going, I'll miss it."

**6.** "Look, I can't jump over them, can I?"

**9.** "Maybe the clock is a little fast . . ."

**10.** "Thank you. Keep the change." "Good trip."

3. "I've got 17 minutes to catch my train."

4. "A red light."

7. "Now a policeman's in our way. He would pick just this time."

8. "What time? . . . 55. It'll leave right under my nose . . ."

11. "Will I make it, or won't I?"

12. "I got it. But that was a close one."
(*Photos by Michel Cambazard*)

63

For an insight into what can be done experimentally with time and place try a sampling of the film library of Cinema 16, a New York film group specializing in unusual, but worthwhile films.

## Angles and How to Use Them

There are, of course, standard definitions for some of the angles used in cinematography. These definitions are arrived at the framing, position, and distance from the camera of the subject. However, like many definitions, these are occasionally vague and often arbitrary. But they help in establishing camera and subject relationship in the script form of the film.

Let's look at some of them.

> **The extreme long shot:** clear only in relation to the long shot.
> **The long shot:** a fairly distant shot of people or scenery giving an overall view of the scene.
> **Medium shot:** one that might frame a subject from head to foot.
> **Medium close-up:** Shows the person from either the knees to the head.
> **The close-up:** From the waist to the head.
> **The extreme close-up:** Only the face, or sometimes only part of the face. It may isolate the batting of an eyelash.

Actually, the precise definition of a shot depends on the one before it and the one after it. What may be a long shot in one scene, may be an extreme long shot in another.

In practical film making there are no definite methods for using the series of shots—although most often they progress from extreme long shot to close-up. You locate the background and then concentrate on the important elements.

The travelogue serves as an example of how the shots can be used in progression. Since the camera leads us into discovery it shows us the overall view of things and then picks out interesting, important details.

Visit a foreign city, Venice perhaps, and the first thing that strikes you is the broad, overall picture of canals, monuments, and buildings. The camera shows us a wide-angle long shot of the Piazza San Marco with pigeons flying, the bold line of the Campanile and all the forms which seem to begin in the sky and end in the water. Then the camera wanders along the small streets and canals, showing us an occasional picturesque silhouette of a passerby, a gondola, and the small shops. As the camera uncovers the real aspect of the city, it comes across interesting details—faces in close-up perhaps. However, adopt this approach with care. A film that varies wide angle views (or long shots) with the precise details of close-ups is much more interesting. You must apply personal judgment even to classic rules.

And it's quite possible to open a scene or even an entire film with a close-up, even an extreme close-up of an object, a hand, a gesture, or a face and follow with a broader shot. You can even go from a medium shot to an extreme close-up to register a sudden reaction, if there's a logical continuity in the idea and in the movement.

Let's leave the travelogue for now and move on to a film that tells a story. Suppose we conjure up a short sequence or situation and write it down cinematographically.

**SUCCESSION OF ANGLES.** — Succession of angles are dictated by the story, by the action or by the imagination of the movie-maker.

**1.** *Extreme Long shot.* — An extreme wide-angle shot (often followed by a pan), similar to this view from high above the piazza San Marco and the gondola harbor, in Venice, is frequently used as a preliminary descriptive shot.

**2.** *Medium shot.* — Our own desire to come near things, to discover them, will guide the camera in a search for angles which are still related to the overall scene, but show the details of form, light and movement.

**3.** *Close-up.* — When nearing the end of its search, the camera moves in for some close-ups. With its space limitations, the close-up is often the most effective way of conveying a human touch or an unexpected image.

*(Photos by Georges Régnier)*

## FROM THE EXTREME LONG SHOT TO THE CLOSE-UP. —

Motion picture terminology to designate various angles definitely lacks precision. Expressions like medium shot or close-up can be interpreted differently according to the technician who uses them. However, people usually agree on the following terms which define the position of the characters in the frame.

A. *Extreme long shot.* — This is the angle used to establish the action in a landscape or against a background. Sometimes the people occupy a very small fraction of the space and are included in it only to establish the dimensions of the scenery. Such a shot will often be taken from above.

B. *Long shot.* — There is a well balanced division of interest between the characters and the scenery. Such a shot is often the starting point or the last image of a camera movement —a pan or a dolly.

C. *Medium shot.* — Here's the "jack-of-all-trades" type of shot. It's the equivalent of a full-size portrait. It frames the characters closely with minimum leeway for the background—used only to back up the action. In a sound film, this is usually the distance at which the dialogue begins.

D. *Medium close-up.* — This shot should frame standing persons from the knee up. It can also frame people at one third of their height and even from the waist up. It's good framing for dramatic dialogue.

E. *Close-up.* — This is the typical frame for one person isolated on the screen or, as in this instance, for a person in relation to another. We find this framing successively used on one, then on the other actor in a still position in a sort of "crossed angle".

F. *Extreme close-up.* — Under this definition we shall find very different framings—face and shoulders, face alone, or even a portion of the face. The extreme close-up makes the most of a look, plays with the many resources of a face, catches the expression of the eyes, the mouth, shows the feeling they convey. We must note here that the direction of the look on the girl's face and the way she is framed relate this shot to the preceding one, although her face is completely isolated on the screen. (*Photos by Michel Cambazard*)

"She made a date with him. He waits for her. The bunch of flowers he holds is rather embarrassing at the moment since she's late. She's not coming, he decides, and starts to leave. He chucks away the flowers and at that moment she arrives. The situation is simple, almost banal but it does leave room for cinematographic invention. Let's see what happens when we write the script for it.

| | |
|---|---|
| *Extreme close-up* | The cart of a flower girl. A bunch of flowers among others. The hand of the saleswoman picks it up. |
| *Close-up with the sales woman barely seen on the side* | The young man takes the bunch of flowers which the woman has wrapped. He pays and leaves. |
| *Medium shot, then close-up (possibly pan)* | He feels very clumsy with the flowers and experiments with the best way to carry it; in front of him, under his arm, or just casually next to him in his hand. He keeps it that way for a while. |
| *Dissolve to long shot* | He arrives at the terrace of a cafe. This is where he is supposed to meet his girl. He chooses a place, puts the flowers on the table with a falsely casual air. The waiter comes by, lifts the flowers delicately in order to wipe the table, then takes the order. |
| *Medium shot and pan* | |
| *Close-up* | The young man looks to the right and to the left, makes sure his girl is not there. He looks at his wrist watch. The waiter returns with his drink. |
| *Medium shot* | The waiter lifts the bouquet again, so as not to ruin it and puts it in the hands of his customer, who looks embarrassed and finally puts it on the chair next to him. The waiter places a glass, a saucer, a pitcher of water, etc. on the table. |
| *Medium close-up* *Dissolve to zoom in to extreme close-up then zoom out to medium closeup* | The young man drinks from his glass, looks around again, looks at the time, drinks again. He puts his glass back on the table. The glass is empty. He looks upset. Obviously she is late. |
| *Medium shot* | Some people come in and sit at the table next to him. At the last moment he rescues the flowers on which a fat gentleman was about to sit. He places the flowers on the table again. |
| *Medium close-up* | He meets the eyes of a young woman who is staring at him. She says a few words (probably about him) to the man who is with her. |
| *Close-up* | The young man places the bunch of flowers on another chair and looks again at his watch. |

| | |
|---|---|
| *Extreme close-up* | His wrist watch indicates 6:05 p.m. |
| *Dissolve to same* | It now indicates 6:25 p.m. |
| *Close-up* | The waiter, idle, is looking at him from the side. |
| *Medium close-up* | The young man calls him, pays his check, gets up and glances toward . . . |
| *Extreme close-up* | The flowers on the chair. |
| *Medium close-up with pan* | He leaves them and goes away. |
| *Medium shot* | The waiter calls him and, with a smile, hands him the bouquet. The other customers on the terrace watch the scene. |
| *Long shot* | The young man walks along the street, sad and discouraged. |
| *Medium close-up* (with pan) | He has forgotten about the flowers which hang from his arm. Suddenly he remembers having them. He sees a woman seated on a bench. He puts the flowers on her knees and walks away. |
| *Long shot* | A young woman—it's "She"—is running toward him. She has seen him from a distance and is calling him. |
| *Close-up with pan* | He turns around, his face brightens, he walks toward her and joins her. She explains volubly why she is late. He doesn't seem ready to show any anger. Suddenly he tells her to wait a minute and leaves the frame. |
| *Medium shot* | He returns hurriedly to the bench and takes back the flowers from the hands of the surprised and indignant woman. |
| *Close-up* | He comes back to his girl. He gives her the flowers. She smiles. They kiss. |
| *Fade Out* | |

We've broken down the scene into many small details and it shows how much freedom one has when dealing a shot-by-shot breakdown of a given situation, intention, or comical effect. Actually, the prop, the flowers, play an important part in the story. It takes on more importance than the characters and is an example of the psychological effect one can achieve by bringing background details into sharp focus.

In the script, the camera is sometimes stationary, sometimes mobile using the pan and the dolly shot. Angle and mobility combine to provide a smooth transition from shot to shot.

The pan can take us from a medium shot to close-up then to a long shot (someone enters a room, pauses in front of the camera, walks away toward a group of people), link an extreme close-up to close-up, or a long shot to medium shot.

BOY MEETS GIRL. — We follow in pictures the script of the scene about the flowers.

1. *Medium close-up.* — The young man and the flower woman. If we have a dolly, or a zoom lens, we can open on the scene with a close-up of the flowers on display, then widen it to show the flower woman presenting a bouquet.

2. *Close-up.* — "These roses will be very becoming to her." This shot could have been tighter, but this way it keeps the flower cart in the frame.

5. *Medium close-up.* — Minutes have passed, very slowly. Will she come? The angle, from the ground up, emphasizes the importance of the bouquet of flowers, which plays an essential part. This picture gives an impression of depth, in the background, the waiter participates fully in the scene.

6. *Extreme close-up.* — He looks at the time once more. He just looked at it two minutes ago. We have here a more subjective framing—that is, we follow the subject more closely. The angle has been chosen to suit the movement of the arm.

**3.** *Medium shot.* — He is very satisfied with the bouquet and a little clumsy carrying it. The shot taken from the ground up suggests a feeling of conquest which the young man may have. At the same time this framing shows the movements of the passers-by.

**4.** *Long shot.* — He chooses a table. The waiter comes over. This situation can be introduced by a short pan which accompanies the young man among the tables and chairs. This angle shows much of the background.

**7.** *Close-up.* — The waiter, idle, looks from the side at this customer who is being stood up. This shot is well balanced with the preceding one, not only in its meaning but also as far as distance and framing are concerned.

**8.** *Medium shot.* — "You forgot something, sir." In this picture, the young man has gotten up and started to leave. The waiter entering the frame from the right has called the man just as he was about to leave the frame, to the left. The tight framing includes the entire scene.

71

**9.** *Long shot.* — He leaves, sad and discouraged, with the useless bouquet hanging from his arm. By shooting this scene from a distance and by emphasizing the background rather than the man, the feeling of loneliness is made more striking.

**10.** *Medium close-up.* — He realizes he still has the flowers, and walks toward the woman seated in the foreground. He hands her the flowers.

**13.** *Medium close-up.* — "Wait a minute, I'll be back." There must be a definite matching in this sequence and those that follow as far as direction is concerned. The young man leaves to the right in this picture, he comes in from the left in the next picture. On the other hand he will leave from the left in picture No. 15 and will enter from the right in picture No 16.

**14.** *Medium shot.* — "Madam, I'm very sorry, but I need my flowers again".
— "What? Listen you . . ." Here's the same angle as in picture No 10. This only emphasizes more clearly the amusing parallel between the two scenes.

**11.** *Long shot.* — A young woman—it is "She"—is running and calling him. In editing it is possible to insert a shot of the young man turning around, his face brightening, and then to come back to the long shot when the girl comes closer.

**12.** *Medium shot.* — "Forgive me, darling, I'm late." — "Not at all . . ."
The two are very much alone despite being surrounded. To convey this idea better, we have picked a bus stop for this scene.

**15.** *Medium shot.* — "You rascal! Ah, young people today . . ." This is a continuation of the preceding shot. It's value lies in the movements and attitudes.

**16.** *Close-up.* — A classical happy ending. Of course, the movement in which he gives her the bouquet, she admires it and smells it, then kisses him, would make it more human and more interesting than can be shown on a still picture.

(*Photos by Michel Cambazard*)

73

The moving shot or pan can be difficult to execute. But the technical inability to make a pan or dolly shot (usually lack of the right equipment) can be overcome by substituting a variety of shots made from several angles. If you don't have a dolly, you can move into a scene by going from long shot to close-up with a series of cuts, each shot made from another angle. What you lose with the technical sophistication of the dolly you make up with the precision and rhythm of the neatly cut shot. Images and words can be used in many ways—provided you know the elementary rules of syntax and grammar.

For example, when you change a shot in a scene from medium to close-up you must change the angle of the camera. Otherwise the result is jumpy, without harmony. If you edit the two shots properly, the cut from one to the other will be experienced but perhaps not even consciously noted by the audience.

You'll have to match the action in your cuts because that important feeling of continuity must be maintained. The cut must pick up the action in a position similar to the one before it. We'll talk much more about this in the section in this chapter on matching action.

## Shots from Above and Below

Shooting from above or below the subject contributes to the expression of an idea. Often, the choice of low or high angle depends on the background. For example, a face looks better against the sky than against the confusion of trees or buildings. A group of people will be more easily distinguished as individuals from a high angle. A high or low angle can contribute to the emotional impact of a shot. A take from above serves to frame objects more tightly, defining their limitations—almost appearing to shrink dimensions. A high angle shot can narrow the limitations of scene almost to the point of giving a claustrophic feeling.

A shot from below appears to widen an image, often conveying a feeling of freedom. In Orson Welles' *Citizen Kane*, a low angle shot was used to convey pride. The low and high angle shot brings out many theological and symbolistic meanings possible with a camera. Even philosophical subtleties of duality of earth and sky occur—but let's not delve too deeply in these nuances.

## Scene Breakdown

Some of the cinematic terminology—angle, matching shot, cut and so on may be a bit confusing. So, perhaps a practical illustration of how all those words are used may be of some help. Let's suppose you write a scene similar to this one:

A vacationing couple, John and Simone, climb a mountain from which they can see a lovely landscape. On top of the mountain they find an orientation table which they study in an attempt to get their bearings. Two other climbers who have reached the top before them show them several landmarks in the distance which they have already identified. After chatting for a time the four leave the mountain together.

One of the essential qualities required of a director is to visualize things easily. Let's forget, the desk we sit at, the four walls surrounding us, and

A SHOT FROM BELOW. — It is often advisable to place the camera slightly below the subject, especially in exterior shooting. In most cases the scene will come out beautifully against one of the best backgrounds there is—This angle appears to widen, to open the image. It is however necessary to be careful about the distortion of line which occurs in shots from below. (*Photo by Georges Régnier*)

imagine that we are at the spot just described. Let's make our actors act just as if they were real, live humans in a real life situation.

| | |
|---|---|
| A.—*Medium shot,* ¾ face, then pan to a *long shot* ¾ from the back, slightly tilted from above. | John and Simone reach the end of the mountain path as they finish their climb. The young woman is out of breath for having hurried on the last steps. They both walk by the camera then walk away toward the orientation table. View of the scenery and of the second couple standing next to the orientation table. |
| B.—*Medium close-up,* then pan until we reach a *close-up,* ¾ face. | John and Simone (taken as they complete their movement) walk near the second couple, go a couple of steps further and stop, one next to the other, in order to admire the scenery. Simone puts her arm on the shoulder of John. Their eyes go from left to right (as seen from the camera). |
| C.—*Long shot* and slow pan | The scenery as it appears to John and Simone: that is, from right to left. |

75

| | |
|---|---|
| D.—*Close-up* changing to *medium close-up* (slightly tilted from above in order to show the top of the orientation table) | We look again at John and Simone. Their eyes are to the right. Simone leads John toward the orientation table. They walk back a few steps. This movement allows us to get in the frame the second couple who makes room for the newcomers next to the orientation table. John looks at it, then points with his finger at one of its indications. |
| E.— *Close-up* | The orientation table. The shadows of John and Simone are projected on it. John's hand points at some indications on the map, then leaves the frame. |
| F.—*Go back to shot D* | We go back to the movement of John as he points in one direction. The young man of the other couple gives him some information. They start talking. They laugh, look again at the scenery for a while, then start to leave together. |
| G.—*Longer shot* *Fade out* | The four of them leave. |

At first glance, the shooting script looks a bit rigid for direct adaptation to actual shooting. And it's true that we'll have to simplify, modify some of the movements. But the work on the script is hardly wasted, since it has forced us to think in cinematic terms.

The scene is now a succession of shots—each designed to do a job. The job may be to bring out a detail or to emphasize a character. The camera, as it changes angle, goes from one position to another, follows the story—establishing the first two main characters, the scenery, and finally the second couple. Its movement and choice of angle is also dictated by the action—the hand which points to the orientation table, for example, and the cut to the distant scenery. The breakdown foresees all the matching action and creates an articulate link between one shot and another, and supplies the basis for editing.

### Cross Cutting

Often we see a scene between two people in conversation. The camera remains in one spot throughout the scene. Actually, the shot reminds us of a still photograph that somehow has been animated. The thinking movie maker takes advantage of the mobility of his camera to make a smooth, lively scene out of what might easily be dull material. Here's how the straight-on conversation shot might be enlivened.

A long shot shows two people approaching each other and at the same time establishes the background. The camera moves in closer to establish a closer link between the two, capturing interesting facial expressions, too. Often the technique of the cross cut will be employed to give the scene pace. It means that first the camera faces one then the other person during the conversation.

CROSS CUTTING. — This technique is often used in professional movies, particularly since the advent of sound pictures. It makes it possible to follow a dialogue between two people talking, both of them framed in relation to the other.

1. *Profile shot.* — This is the classical angle for two people talking.

2. *Close-up shot.* With second person seen in the frame from the back. The person facing us is on the right side of the frame, seen from above the shoulder of the man he is talking to. The latter is on the left of the image. We must direct the person facing us to look toward the camera.

3. *Reverse shot.* Now the person who faces us is on the left side of the frame, his partner being placed on the right. It is advisable for such shots to keep the camera at the same distance from the subject.
(*Photos by Georges Régnier*)

But, in each case, as it centers upon one character, it retains a portion of the other person involved (the photos, page 77, illustrate this point). This maintains both characters in proper relationship to each other.

In this kind of cross cutting, the camera remains in the same relation to both characters. While one looks toward the center of the screen from the left, the other looks at it from the right. As a matter of fact, their eyes seem to meet at the center of the screen. If one is photographed from the back from the right side, the other is shot from the back on the left side. This is a technique you may find applicable in any number of conversation scenes—people seated at a table, around a desk, under an umbrella.

(It should be noted that modern technique often calls for longer scenes with fewer cuts and less changes of angle. Movement is provided by action of the characters in relation to a fixed camera position.)

This same technique can be applied to filming fixed objects in a landscape by means of the pan shot. A long pan, taking in one object after another might prove rather dull. It also resembles someone turning his head constantly without ever reaching the point from which he started. Instead of a steady pan, interrupt it with a pause that allows the audience to inspect the object more closely, before going on to the next one.

### Matching Action

There are at least two types of matching action—both tremendously important to film making.

Matching direction: In a fast action sequence composed of many short takes (a race or skiers going down a hillside, for example) the result will be more strongly unified and less confusing to the audience if the subject always moves in the same direction. If a skier whizzes out of the frame from the left, he should reenter from the right. Of course, we can change the direction of the action while it takes place in the frame. The skier can enter from the right, make a turn and exit to the right. In the next frame he must come from the left to maintain the new direction. In any event, once you establish the action going in one direction, you must maintain that direction unless you let the audience know that there's been a change. This is called matching direction and the Western horse opera with its perennial chase is one of the most elementary examples of how it's used. The sense of direction or change of direction are faithfully followed so that the viewer really feels in the midst of the action.

If you watch closely enough, you'll notice that the pursuers and pursued always cross the same frame, turn around the same tree, shake the same branch as they dash by, or skid in the same way on the same sharp turn. The cut to first one crossing an easily identifiable spot and then a cut to those following gives the audience some idea of the tightness of the race. It's simple—but effective cinema.

On the other hand, with an action composed of multiple scenes which take place far apart in time (a car trip, for example) it's better to vary the direction of the image from one take to another. Shots can dissolve into each other to maintain continuity (see chapter on special effects).

MATCHING OF DIRECTION. — In order that a movement be easily followed from one image to another, it must be matched in direction.

1. The skier enters from the *right* side of the frame.

2. He crosses the frame *from right to left*.

3. He goes out of the frame on the *left side*.

4. In the next picture, the skier will enter the frame on the opposite side from which he left (here on the *right*).

5. The skier is free to turn around. The movement then changes direction.

6. The skier leaves the frame on the *right*. In the following frame, he should therefore come in from the left.

Matching movement: If you walked onto the set of a studio it wouldn't take long for you to realize that the key word in one day's shooting is "match." Sample conversation might sound like this:

Director: We'll match it when he gets up.

Script girl: The movement of his arms doesn't match.

Cameraman: Does this match the night scene?

Editor: It is impossible to match this. He didn't make the same move.

Director: (to the script girl) If the matching isn't any good we'll have to reshoot.

What's all the noise about matching? All it is, really, is similarity between a movement made at the end of one shot to the same movement on the following take, so that passage from shot to shot is smooth. It means that it's always necessary to repeat the same action on both shots so that the editor can match the shots perfectly. Here's an example of how it works.

A close-up shows an actor in conversation and then getting up and going to the door.

In the next take, a long shot, the actor walks toward the door, opens it and walks out.

The movement of the actor arising is recorded on both shots and in editing

MATCHING DIRECTION. — The different shots which compose a scene must give a feeling of continuity.

1. *Long shot.* — Here horseback riders practice. Whether you shoot this with the camera fixed or with a panning action, it will show the horses moving from right to left.

2. *Medium shot* (Profile). — We can come closer to the subject if we like as long as the movement of the horses remains the same: from right to left.

5. *Long shot.* — The riders are starting a change in direction. Naturally in the next frame the direction of the horses will be the same.

6. *Medium shot.* — The riders are now going to leave the frame on the right. They must enter the next picture from the left.

**3.** *Medium shot* (¾ face). — The passage between one shot and the next will be made smooth and pleasant at the time of editing, even if the angle is entirely different, as long as the matching of movement and direction are observed.

**4.** *Medium shot* (¾ back) — The matching of movement between this picture and the preceding one must take into account the rhythm of the trotting horses.

**7.** *Medium shot* (¾ back). — The matching of direction with the preceding shot has been well made. If you look closely you will see that even the movements of the legs of the grey horse match perfectly.

**8.** *Extreme long shot.* — The angle of the camera and the distance of the shot are very different here from the preceding image, but the direction of movement has been matched. These two shots can very well come right next to each other at the time of the editing.

*(Photos by Michel Cambazard)*

81

MATCHING OF MOVEMENT. — The rhythmic movements of the Bedouin woman made interesting footage. The fact that the movement of the woman who repeated regularly made it easier to match movement both in the medium shot and in the close-up. Both these shots match, although it is possible to detect some difference between them. Notice how the editing of the two shots would have been smoother if the angle of the camera had been more radically changed from one shot to the other.

(*Photos by Georges Régnier*)

the sequence the movement begins in the close-up and the first frame of the long shot will show the same rising movement in precisely the same position. The viewer's eye, having followed the movement, is transported smoothly through the matching shots almost without being conscious about it.

The action, of course, can be more complicated, necessitating the reshooting of several individual movements. Where the shots will be cut together depends on the editor.

The problem of matching has several aspects. For example, if we see an actor walk through a door with a coat and hat on, and carrying a cane, it follows that in the next shot showing him in the street he can't be wearing a jacket, with no hat, and carrying an umbrella.

Another important point in matching scenes is the time of day in one shot in relation to the time in another shot. One scene can't be dark and the next sunny if the shots are supposed to take place at the same time. It's up to the cameraman (and everyone else concerned) to make sure that the lighting matches in shots that are to be cut together.

But it's the script girl who has the major responsibility for seeing to it that things match in professional films. Did he wear the hat or did he carry it? Was the cigarette just lit or was it half smoked, Did he hold his glass in his right or in his left hand? Was the glass full or empty? The script girl has to keep track of many, many minor details that can turn out to be major errors—the kind that people write to movie columnists about.

It's not uncommon for a still shot to be made at the end of a scene, with everything in precisely the exact spot occupied at the end of the shot. Polaroid cameras are often used because of the speedy result. The still picture supplies a permanent, accurate record.

But no matter how you do it, with a still camera or just notes written on a slip of paper, you'll have to take care to match your shots—or editing is liable to be an essay into mental torture.

## Sequence Continuity

You should never underestimate the importance of sequence continuity during the shooting of a film. Each take must fit into the next so that they constitute a scene. And the various scenes must be linked together to comprise a sequence of scenes—or the sum of your film.

This building of a film, almost brick by brick as you would a house, is primarily a part of editing—but is also a part of shooting. Even if there was no need for a scene to match action with the next in a mechanical sense, there would nevertheless be a similarity in image or idea, or sometimes in effect of contrast.

In the 1920's, it was cinematically fashionable to match similar objects— the wheel of the automobile dissolved into a roulette wheel at Monte Carlo, bubbling water from a ship's propeller dissolved into water running from a faucet, and so on. But today, image matching for continuity has developed along other lines utilizing straight cuts. Here are some examples of how a cut might be made today.

Contrast in camera movement: Pan shot up into the sun from one scene, and down from the sun to the next shot. A zoom toward an object or face, followed by a zoom away.

Alternate movement: A man walks away from the camera. In the next shot he moves toward it.

Linking ideas: A travel poster followed by a shot of a road as a car travels over it. A close-up of a perspiring man, followed by a scene of waves breaking on a shore.

Contrast: An extreme long shot followed by an extreme close-up. A crushed cigarette smoldering in an ash tray and then a shot of a tree branch moving in the wind.

Contrast by omission: a man drives off in a new car and the same car towed back by a wrecker.

This type of linking of shots should never look artificial. It must take place naturally in the course of the story and not slow it down. A dissolve can serve to emphasize the effect (dissolves are described in chapter on special effects).

## Image Composition

When you compose an image the intent is to give the lines and masses in the scene a balance so as to emphasize the main subject, to create a picture that speaks for itself. It is much the same thing strived for in still photography. But with motion pictures we have the added element of movement. Composition must never inhibit movement, since that is the main business of films. A spontaneous shot, with plenty of movement is much preferable to a stilted, elaborately composed scene.

In setting the composition for your scene, don't stand off too far from your subject, or you may bury an important gesture. Frame it tightly, with just enough margin for safety around the important action. Don't allow empty meaningless "air" to creep into a scene. Of course, in a long shot of a landscape, you'll be shooting from quite a distance compared to other shots, but make sure that lines and masses are clearly defined. Remember that a vast expanse of scenery is going to be compressed into the narrow confines of a screen. This means loss of detail—particularly with 8mm. Look for the important features —lines, masses, good shadows and contrasting highlight areas. After the long shot, move in for a close-up of important details, taking advantage of your equipment's mobility to change angle.

And here's where the depth of field of your normal or wide-angle lens can really do a job for you. At f/5.6 or smaller openings depth of field when filming long shots with the lens set at infinity or slightly less, is extremely large. This means that you can get foreground objects in sharp focus to give your scenes a feeling of real depth. An object in the foreground holds the eye, and even pushes the background farther away, suggesting depth and spaciousness. The passage of an object or person through the foreground in a dolly or pan shot gives a three-dimensional feeling to the shot. Even when the object fails to register sharply on the film it will serve its purpose, since the attention of the viewer is held by the main subject. It helps, though, to keep slightly out-of-focus objects in the corner of the frame or in a shadow area.

Conversely, a close-up can be more effective when the background is not out of focus. Either use your depth of field scale to throw the background completely out of focus or use a neutral background such as the sky. Above all, try not to have any identifiable moving objects in the background. They distract the viewer and take his attention from the main subject.

A film image is a fleeting one. Thus, its meaning must be projected in clearly understood terms. Its main point of interest must be clearly emphasized, with movement, face or object designed to hold the audience's attention. The eye, in looking at a picture for the second time, will focus on a detail noticed on first viewing. If it happens to be a crowd shot, the viewer is almost certain to pick out one face in the crowd and return to it the second time. It might be that the face is better framed or more interestingly lit than other faces, or it was the only face the viewer had time to see. You can take advantage of this if the face is the most important one by making sure that it stands out—by using lighting, position, or fast cutting coupled with the kind of composition that forces the viewer to see it. Of course, not everything can be controlled and the element of change always seems to play a part in motion pictures.

THE CHOICE OF ANGLE. — With any subject, for example the Chateau and park at Versailles, you will always be confronted with the problem of choosing the best camera angle, depending on what effect you want to make. These two pictures of Versailles show exactly the same thing. The point of view differs only because one angle is slightly upwards, the other downwards (the difference between the two positions of the camera is 5 feet. But the result is quite different).

This shot from above is more complete, more architecture conscious. The position and the harmony of the building are better served. If the park were to become suddenly filled with visitors, this would be the angle to choose. However, the picture above has more lightness, more elegance, and one seems to imagine a silhouette standing at the top of the stairs . . .
(Photos by Ghislain Cloquet)

A scene in a war film might show a group of soldiers marching to the front. Suddenly, a dog dashes out, following the troops. The dog captures the audience—although it provided only a minor sidelight in the scene.

## Technique and Expression

It's important to master the technique of making motion pictures so that you can predict results with a fair degree of certainty. However, there are times when the film maker should discard technique. Above all, he should know how to present his films so that the audience isn't conscious of devices, methods, and invention. Technique can be so overpowering that it takes the place of expression in importance. Don't load your film with technical effects. They may be admirable, but they can slow your film and hide your meaning. By unnecessary technique I mean camera angles that strive too hard for effect, tricky framing, overly elaborate foregrounds, and unneeded camera movements.

The technique should always be subordinate to what you are trying to say. You better have a reason for getting so close to a subject that even the pores of his skin are sharply defined, or shooting from above a crowd to show only the top of heads. Dramatic or humorous intention must be the guide. If you zoom, pan or dolly away from or into a subject it must contribute to showing a gesture or following a movement or emphasizing a detail, or broadening the view after an action has been completed. The sheer desire to zoom, pan or dolly isn't enough.

Your job is to make people forget about your presence behind the camera, to forget the camera itself. When you show off your technical virtuosity you break the magic charm of motion pictures because the audience suddenly is aware of contrivance—wants to know how it was done. An obvious technical effect is just as disturbing as the passerby who decides to stare right into your lens while you are shooting.

Many people are quite sincere when they tell a film creator that his photography is beautiful. Frankly, I find it no compliment. If people are captured by the beauty of the image, it may be that the meaning of the film itself wasn't important enough to hold them.

A good film should primarily arouse an emotional response—and only as an afterthought admiration for technical skill. Technique should be subordinate to ideas—at their service and for use in as flexible a manner as possible. A sequence will be successful if the shooting script makes it possible to easily follow the action. This means that various ideas are well linked, there are no bad cuts or unpleasant changes of direction, and at no time is the viewer conscious of the hand of the director, framing, editing or lighting.

Charley Chaplin is aware of all those things and his films show it. They were created with simple techniques and say what they have to say in clear, direct terms. They will never get out of date or old fashioned.

What's inside the frame is more important than how it got there. There are films that were shot quickly—without elaborate planning at all—but whose interest is tremendous because of the documentary material filmed. However, most often, a good film is a combination of emotional values and the best method for projecting those values.

## The Set

Any set is adequate—it's the way that you use it that counts. You don't have to build sets even if the material and financial means are at hand. And why should you—when even the major companies are discarding the artificiality of the studio and going out to real locations?

The theater set is easy to make because the stage properties only suggest something for the audience's imagination to develop into a feeling of reality. Motion picture sets must be true to life—must never look artificial. The studios usually call in professionals—a lot of them. You can do just as well with what already exists. In fact, the best studio set is rarely as effective as the real thing. The studio offers an easy out because the set can be constructed anywhere in a time-space sense. But the chances are you won't be faced with constructing a set for a historical film set in remote parts of the world.

PORT OF SHADOWS, Marcel Carne (1938). — You may have seen this film and remember the beautiful scenes and spellbinding settings. A typical background is shown in this photograph—desolate piece of land, a corner of a harbor in the background, a pile of wood refuse, a pale winter sun, a cloud of smoke in the sky, an over-all cast of grey. It creates the feeling of emptiness toward which the characters are walking. (*Photo by Sofradis*)

Do you need a street corner, an ivy covered wall, a street light? They are a lot easier to find than a castle. For interior shots, you can use a bedroom, library, attic or living room. Your own home, or the homes of friends are bound to be available. Certainly, some technical problems will crop up—but a little imagination and you'll solve them.

The really important consideration is the style of the set. It must contribute to the mood you want to create in a given sequence. Here, you're two people—the director who evaluates the aesthetic value of the set and the cameraman who judges its practicality. A look through your camera viewfinder will help determine the best possible shooting angles and where and how to place your characters.

The next problem is lighting. Occasionally, the set itself will suggest lighting arrangements. An idea for a film can be born through the atmosphere of a place. Its people, objects, smells, can contribute ideas. Even familiar environments, the city or street in which you live, can make a film and provide tailor-made sets.

*La Bete Humaine* (from a novel by Emile Zola) tells the story of only a few people. But above all, it tells the story of the poetry of railroad tracks extending

THE HUMAN BEAST, Jean Renoir (1938). — The setting and the characters are intimately tied together to create atmosphere. The grimy faces of Jean Gabin and Carette, their worn work clothes, are one with the locomotive. They seem to belong to it as much as the riveted metal plates. (*Photo by Lux-Films*)

toward the horizon, monstrous locomotives, railroad stations, dark embankments, and smoke darkened landscapes.

*Quai des Brumes* (Port of Shadows) evokes the nostalgia of a harbor, its ships whistles singing of travel, and a place where the actual sea is never seen. *La Strada* tells the story of a road, white and gray, but leads into a distance that has nothing at the end. These films have been made because of a particular piece of scenery—or more precisely because of the poetry of the scenery. Look around you—the places you know have their own secret meaning and can be used to tell a world of stories.

I know several movie makers who carry their cameras almost everywhere they go—shooting away like mad at almost everything that moves. They return home and lock up the camera—never shooting a single frame of the youngster next door who is getting married, or the policeman on the beat, or the man who runs the corner grocery. These things, which compose the life around them, might make the material for a superb film.

A survey of the things around you can lead to some really good sets—and unselfconscious actors—a sunny school room filled with children, the place you work and its desks covered with outlines, sketches, bills and designs, a print shop around the corner, the local garage, or an old country house with an air of mystery.

You can find backgrounds at the country club, golf course, race track, tennis

UNCONSCIOUS ACTORS. — This couple has obviously not noticed the camera. The attitude, although simple and classic, would probably not look natural if it had been practiced.

*(Photo by Georges Régnier)*

court, locker rooms, ski lodge, or any other place where the story of an athlete can be told.

And let the set speak for itself. Look for the out of the way corners that tell more than words, that are symbols which you can give meaning to with your camera.

Even the more sparse modern design type of background can provide an interesting set. Its clean lines, bright objects, and unusual shapes may be just the thing for your film.

But no matter what type of set you chose, remember that the set is not a static thing. It has a life of its own.

### Actors

Actually, I should not use the term actors—but rather people because you should use only those people in your film who can project an idea with conscious posturing.

We are all unconscious actors. The trick is to capture the "act" in its most natural form. You want a glimpse of real life. The professional actor's aim is to create something that looks quite natural—but without apparent intent. This is one reason why children, people who have not been excessively exposed to civilization, and animals are the best actors. They don't react to the camera as does the average person. There is no stiffening, posturing, or retreat behind a mask.

Let's take another look at the comparison between the legitimate stage and motion pictures. The actor creates his character right on stage in the legitimate theater. We tend to forget that we watch an actor and immerse ourselves in the fiction he develops. On the screen the actor must live his part. He is actually the presence rather than an imitation. That's why in front of the motion picture camera a part must be lived and felt, rather than acted. The professional is often "typed." That is, he plays a particular kind of part that audiences expect. *Unconscious actors.* The amateur film is more likely to be concerned with people doing things that they normally do, than with real or attempted acting. In the recording of personal events family and friends take the place of actors. The travelogue records the actions of people who just happen to be around. The documentary and the newsreel cameraman are more concerned with attitudes, work, and individual effort than with posturing.

The camera, in many amateur films, is similar to the artist who quickly sketches an expression, a movement, or a gesture, almost as soon as it happens. The camera is the eye which records human life, quickly, discreetly. It must look without being seen.

This capturing of actuality is the aim of almost every movie maker. But it's not easy to work without attracting attention. The pro is particularly handicapped. He rarely works alone and his equipment is bound to attract attention. In order to get away with this "candid type" of shooting, the pro often disguises his camera. In the French film, *Monsieur Ripois,* Gerard Philipe wanders the streets of London. Some of the shots were made from a doorway, with the camera half hidden by a newspaper. This way the curious weren't alerted to the fact that a film was being made and it was quite possible to get the footage without interference.

The popularity of French star Jean Gabin almost made it impossible to shoot in Genoa for a film called *Au Dela des Grilles* by Rene Clement. Crowds followed Gabin everywhere. What Clement did was send a crew to a remote part of the city, have them pretend to shoot, and attract the crowd away so that the needed shots could be made.

For another film shot in a city, a rude shack was erected and left long enough to get passersby used to it. Then a camera was emplaced and shooting done through a specially prepared hole.

Since the amateur can act with a great deal more unobtusiveness than the pro (mainly because of the smaller bulk of his equipment) he can use his camera reportorially, with much greater facility. *Improvised actors:* In filming fiction, you'll have to use people to conform to the requirements of the story. Thus, candid shooting techniques won't be of much help. Unless you are of the more persuasive type, you'll not be working with professional actors—so you enlist friends and family. It might be a good idea to limit your script in respect to the number of people you'll need to shoot the film. In trying to visualize the best types for your script, don't think of physical appearance alone. Instead, think of how the people you know may react to particular situations in the script. As we've noted, the motion picture actor is often a type or character. That's one reason that professional films can often employ a complete un-

FOUR BAGS FULL, Claude Autant-Lara (1956). — A motion picture actor represents, above all, a "presence." Here are Jean Gabin and Bourvil, easily recognizable. However, beyond their own personality, we can see the types they portray. Their physical appearance, their temperament, the behavior which we expect of them, constitute the character of the film.   (Photo by Franco-London Film)

known. He fills a certain preconception of what a character should be. Or, parts are custom tailored to the actor—because he is expected to do certain things, to react, to look, to be along the lines of a well defined pattern.

You can do much the same thing with your friends. Among them you may be able to find people who'll fit exactly into the parts that you have created—or create the parts to fit the people you have available.

It will take lots of patience to make your people forget the camera. I've found camera conciousness as far away as Africa. If one of the local people had traveled to Europe during his period of military service he quite naturally recognized the camera. The reaction might be to snap to attention and salute. The usual approach was to ask the former soldier to perform some casual, familiar every day action. After a time he would forget the camera.

Actually, people who live by instinct make fine actors. Also, you'll find that those who avoid contact with large numbers of people and have not developed superficial personalities make good actors, too. The latter type may include anyone who works under fairly solitary conditions—a farmer, or a scientist, or a fisherman, for example. People who are exposed to motion pictures often feel that movie acting means hiding their real personalities—perhaps because they are shy or as a means of defense. It takes a lot of work to get to act naturally—and quite often the work shows.

THE BAKER'S WIFE, Marcel Pagnol (1939). — Raimu was the prototype of the born actor, the great actor. With a consummate skill in his movements and his face expressions, sometimes overdoing them, he succeeded in creating a character who is more true to life than reality itself. This is because he had the ability to keep contact with reality, and when he over-emphasized it was only in the creation of a type.                                        (Photo by Cie Méditerranéenne de Films)

You'll also encounter the born actor—the man or woman who can assume any role and who can accentuate what really is a normal expression or emotion. They never give the impression that they are performing for the camera.

The first job of the director is to overcome the stiffness of movement and the side long glances at the camera that seem to be part and parcel of the amateur actor.

And strangely enough, the next problem may be to overcome an opposing fault—the obviously forced attempt at being natural. This is usually typified by the overly done gesture so beware of an overabundance of hand movements. Your actor just may be tempted to do much more than you ask of him. You might try explaining it this way: The actor must not think about what he is doing—he should just do it.

The best kind of script calls for people who do things familiar to your actors. If you ask your actors to do the unfamiliar things in an unfamiliar environment they just won't be at ease. Your cast will be much more at home around a campfire than portraying a group of gangsters. As an aside, it might be best to leave gangster movies to the pros.

While you don't have the resources—material or financial—of the professional, you can exercise some of his prerogatives in choosing people whose physical makeup will make the character they are portraying more believable.

FARREBIQUE, Georges Rouqier (1947). — In the character of the grandfather in this poetic treatment of peasant life, we are seeing the very opposite of acting. We are dealing with a real man whose everyday gestures have been captured by the director and left in their original background. This old farmer is the prototype of the improvised actor.     (Photo by Ecran Francais, Films Etienne Lallier)

Couple facial characteristics with the right background and good lighting and you'll have a convincing character. As a matter of fact, how about the director who comes across just the face he needs on a bus, at a soda fountain, or behind a counter? He finds just what he needs—as large, or even larger than life. Occasionally, the "character" is almost unreal—something like an exaggerated copy of life.

Don't expend your energies attempting to get ordinary people to ape Hollywood mannerisms. As we said, make the character fit the natural bent of your amateur actor. The Italian films owe much of their charm to the fact that they present faces that don't have that professional appearance. Quite often complete unknowns are used to project their own personalities. Outstanding examples of the success of this technique are "Man of Aran" by Robert Flaherty and "Farrebique" by Rougier. Look for your people in the life you know best and stick close to the line of reality.

## Makeup and Costumes

This section has a logical relation to the preceding one. It actually emphasizes much the same thing. We no more like easily spotted makeup in films than do we care for false displays of emotion. Professional films do use makeup but not to the extent generally believed. So much has been written about these physical

**93**

A PRISONER OF WAR HAS ESCAPED, Robert Bresson (1956). — Robert Bresson spent a long time searching for faces that would fit his idea of the characters, and he refused to use professional actors. The hero of the film is a student whose interpretation was scene by scene created by the director. To this degree the production is a sort of amateur film—also a film of genius.     (Photo by Gaumont)

transformations that the average movie goer is quite sure that anything connected with motion pictures is artificial. This, at the very least, is an exaggerated attitude.

If the early morning makeup ritual is sacred to Hollywood, then it's equally true that a great many faces appear on the screen with little or no makeup. A femine face may employ all the tricks in the cosmetic box to make it even more lovely. But actually, this is the extent of much screen makeup. Many actors use no makeup at all.

It is a good idea to use slightly orange makeup for black-and-white films to prevent excessive paleness in contrast to dark clothes and background objects. The face shine that used to be taboo in the past is quite acceptable today. It's even advisable when dealing with male actors since it gives a greater sense of reality.

For color film, makeup is even closer to reality—departing little from what the average woman wears in every day life.

Let's leave wigs, false beards and the like in the shop window and stick to the reality of the human face as it really is—with its natural beauty and its faults, too.

About the best approach to costume films is not to approach them at all. For dress in your films, take a look at the clothes people wear every day—and make those your costumes. It's the best way.

CHAPTER 6

# Exteriors

Until now we've examined just about everything that's connected with the preparation needed to make a film, and to a certain extent to the technique required by the amateur. We'll take a look at the job of the sound technician and the editor later on. For now, let's get down to the business of actually making a motion picture. Experience, and the problems that arise through actually doing things, are the best teachers.

We'll start with outdoor shooting. It's somewhat easier than shooting indoors and probably is the favorite working area of most amateurs. Outdoor shooting provides a lot of the film making drive and opportunity for using one's camera in the first place. We'll be concerned with black-and-white film for now, and take up color shooting in another chapter.

## Getting Ready for Production

We might use the case of a film that tells a fiction story, since this implies the most difficult type of movie. If you plan to shoot it in the summer, you may have spent the winter working on a script, discussed it with the people who will help you, and have a final shooting script. The time approaches to translate all the work and planning into film. Equipment has been checked, with all the things you'll need gathered into one place where they'll be easy to reach. But let's leave all the neat leather gadget bags where they are for now and think a bit about the location. Of course, you can pack up, go out and find a place that looks like it might do and start shooting by whatever light nature decides to supply. But, if you want to get the most out of any given background it's best to do a little advance scouting.

Devoting a few days to choosing a background offers several advantages. You'll be able to think of the background in terms of shooting angles, for one thing. Outdoors, one finds a multitude of choices as far as attractive scenery goes—in fact, too many choices. You look at all outdoors and feel that's all too much. You can't possibly cram everything onto a movie frame, and you'll have to be selective. This business of selection represents the first job in choosing a location.

Even sites you know well, the place at which you spent a vacation perhaps, should be investigated carefully from the cameraman's point of view. Memory, even a fresh one, is quite different from the camera eye. Your camera can be employed as a tool in determining the right location. It will make it possible to find really good shooting angles and to decide which will be the ones you'll use to make the film say what you wish to say. There are small, handy instruments called director's finders that can be adjusted to match the focal length of a variety of lenses. Most professional motion picture equipment firms sell them. Lacking the director's finder, use the viewfinder of your camera.

And in looking over a location you'll have to take into account the effect that light has on it. Light strikes objects differently. The effect it has on a stone is different than its effect on a tree, or hills, or the front of an old house. It depends on the time of day, the time of the year, the color of the sky, and the object itself.

In fact, light is the main thing you'll be concerned with in looking for the right shooting angles for your film. For example, a group of historic ruins that fit neatly into your script may look best in the morning sun, or perhaps the light only reaches an important narrow street in a small village about noon, or maybe it's the evening sun that makes a distant mountain range look absolutely stunning against the gray and blue of the sky.

Thus, for each site you choose, you'll also have to take into consideration the best direction and time of day for the light. You may be able to shoot one sequence in the morning and another in the afternoon. For a long sequence, involving a variety of shooting angles, you may have to work several mornings or several afternoons to complete the footage in the same kind of light.

This is the kind of thing that leads to a work schedule so that you'll be able to use your time in the most efficient manner. You may even go so far as to create a shooting schedule—an invaluable thing if you're dealing with many people, a variety of costumes, several spots where action takes place, and many props. This is the task of the assistant director on a professional location. It's actually an orderly recapping, based on the various shooting sites, of the numbers on the shooting script which correspond to the background, actors involved, costumes each wears, props, time of action, and other details. This shooting schedule must be kept up to date. If it receives the right amount of attention it will go a long way in preventing you from forgetting things.

While these preparations seem rather elaborate, in the opinion of most directors, a film is nothing but the execution of carefully prepared plans. But, by all means, keep the schedule within bounds. Make it conform to your particular needs without becoming so involved as to be more inhibiting than useful.

## Matching the Light

The choice of location, and the time of day that you use it is based on the light quality and the particular time of day when it most serves the purposes of your film. In previous paragraphs I suggested that long sequences be shot over a period of two or more days. I'd like to go one step further along those lines and emphasize the importance of matching the light from shot to shot. I've seen amateur films where several shots in a sequence were obviously shot under a variety of lighting conditions—where the intensity and even the direction of the light varied considerably. It's even rather common to see two cuts where one was shot under a bright, sunny sky while the second was filmed under a gray, overcast sky. It seems a bit weak to justify this by saying the

ONE LANDSCAPE, TWO LIGHTS. — A landscape is to a large extent what the light makes it. This quiet bay at the foot of the mountains has a completely different aspect, depending on whether it is indirectly lit (picture on the left) or bathed in the sun (picture on the right). In the first instance, it looks wild, mysterious, while in the other it is more pleasant and charming but lacks mystery and originality. *(Photos by Jacques Boulas)*

weather was against you. Actually, there's no urgency to maintain schedule that forces the amateur to shoot at all costs. In fact, a really fine film can be ruined because someone was impatient enough not to wait for the right light.

*Matching the light is almost as important as matching the action.* You just can't begin a sequence with contrasty light that makes sharp highlights and deep shadows and follow it with a shot in flat light from a gray sky—unless you purposely want to show a changing sky with clouds intermittently covering and uncovering the sun. While it's quite annoying to halt shooting to wait for the sun to come out from behind the clouds—you can wait all day—this is something you'll have to do if your film is to have photographic continuity.

Watch a professional crew at work and you'll see them watching the direction of the clouds through tinted glass in order to be prepared for the most favorable shooting time. These people are conditioned to expect a certain continuity and unity of lighting in each sequence—even if not consciously aware of it. Only when you make sure that the light is right will this continuity be present in your films.

Does this mean that good footage can only be made under bright sunlight? Hardly. An overcast sky may mean the difference between a dull shot and an interesting landscape. A brooding sky may instill a sense of tragedy in your film. Or, it may be that rain will provide the very background you need to project a feeling. However, in these cases you still must maintain the continuity of lighting from one of the sequences to the other. Paradoxically, that old sun may be the undoing of your shooting schedule.

Matching light is a must in two connected shots, particularly if the shooting angle varies little between them. For example, if you follow a medium close-up of a group of people with a tight close-up of only one of the group the same lighting should be used for both shots. If in the first shot the group is under the slight shadow of a tree, don't shoot the tight close-up in bright sunlight. And it's undoubtedly true that professional films often observe this rule in the breach. You may see a long shot lit by subdued light with a closer shot employing an elaborate lighting setup completely unrelated to the first shot.

## Reflectors

Sunlight, incomparable and irreplaceable for long shots is rarely the best for close-ups of people's faces. It creates heavy shadows and emphasizes the harshness of features. It's best to use direct sunlight when it comes from the side, or at a three-quarter angle from the back of the subject—or even completely from the back. If you use the backlight, you can soften the shadows it causes in faces by redirecting light with a reflector. Often, a natural object—water, sand, a white wall, or even the sky or clouds can serve as a reflector. If there's no way of taking advantage of already existing, natural reflectors, try a man-made reflector. Pros use wood panels about three feet square covered with silver foil. Actually, one side is brightly polished and the other dull. You can use the silver foil on one side and a flat white paint on the other. This provides two very different intensities of light. The reflector should be supported by some type of stand or tripod. A three foot square panel may be a bit bulky but you can make it more portable by cutting it in half and connecting the two halves with hinges that make it possible to fold the reflector rather compactly. Or, you can use somewhat smaller panels or a white sheet that can be rolled up and stored easily.

Reflectors can be a bit hard to take. The light they throw into an actor's face is hot and uncomfortable and often electric lights may be substituted by the pros. However, that means power and it just might not be handy. It's a good idea to keep reflector use to a minimum—only where actually needed and for the briefest possible time.

Reflectors also present the problem of keeping them steady. Since you'll usually need them to throw light into a subject's face, the height of a reflector must be constant—something difficult to maintain on a windy day. Good, solid reflector stands are your best bet. Above all, don't use mirrors for reflectors since they create definite, almost uncontrollable hotspots. Did I say never? Well, hardly ever. A mirror can be just the thing to get light into an

REFLECTING SCREENS. — Here is a scene from a professional movie, as seen by the crew. You can see the type of reflectors commonly used. They would be bulky for the amateur movie maker. However, any wide, flat surface provides an even amount of reflected light. *(Photo from the work on the film "Combat pour Tous," Georges Régnier)*

USE OF REFLECTORS. — Reflectors were used in this picture because the light from the sky comes from behind the actors. The light reflected by the screens softens the shadows and gives more detail to the image. The young girl, who has to look toward the screens, is obviously bothered by the extreme light they create. *(Photo by Georges Régnier)*

archway or into a background interior in an exterior-interior shot.

Another inexpensive piece of equipment you want is a simple bit of fabric (6 x 6 ft.) to act as a diffusor for close-ups. The cloth can be mounted on a frame to hold it in position. The cloth, used in place of the reflector, scatters the light rather than concentrates it.

This set of diffusors and reflectors represent a rather comprehensive list of devices that aid in achieving the ultimate in correct lighting. They help in overcoming some of the difficulties that are bound to arise when you depart from the field of the documentary, newsreel, or family film. You can get by without them providing you choose your lighting conditions with extra care. Light and shadow must be balanced and as I've mentioned, the best light is that coming from the side—from a three-quarter angle—or even from behind the subject. Unless you are looking for some special effect, avoid shooting around noon. Vertical light tends to shrink shadows. Confine shooting to either morning or late afternoon. But in planning a series of shooting days remember that the screen image does not exist in a vacuum. Rather, it is related to the preceding and following images. So again, I emphasize the importance of matching light from shot to shot since good lighting is not only important for best visual effect, but in the editing stage it makes possible the logical interweaving of a series of shots. The photographic element must make its contribution to the unity of time and action.

I've mentioned this business of shooting with the light behind the subject for either a silhouette effect or when using reflectors or diffusors to fill in detail. You'll have to protect your lens from flare with either a matte box or a lens shade. If those aren't available, a piece of cardboard or wood held over the lens will do. The object is to prevent stray light rays from sneaking into the lens and causing flare on the frame edges. Be particularly careful during panning that light can't strike directly on the lens. A screen or filter over the lens can be of help, too.

## Filters

Black-and-white film renders the world of color in terms of gray. Since we've been exposed to black-and-white photography almost since birth, we learn to accept it. Color filters make it possible to play with and change the various elements on the gray scale—to accent, to differentiate between two similar colors, to darken, or to lighten.

For example, the medium yellow filter (K2) is used most often to stop part of the blue light in the atmosphere from reaching the film. Used for a sky shot, it darkens the sky and makes the white clouds stand out strongly. Without the medium yellow filter a blue sky would reproduce as a very light gray on film with little differentiation from dead white.

In much the same way, a medium green filter is used for a shot where green is the dominant color in a scene. While it doesn't eliminate green, it does result in greens reproduced as a lighter gray than without the filter. A stronger green filter makes the effect even more marked—with the correction taking on the form of interpretation to emphasize some colors while doing away with others.

Orange and red filters provide an even more noticeable effect. Blue sky and green grass reproduces as much denser grays than without these filters. The use of filters can be rather startling—setting up strong gray tones in opposition to white ones to emphasize clouds, reflections, or the rays of the sun. Filters are actually a reflection of photographic style—but should not be used indiscriminately. The use of filters should be in keeping with the mood. For example, a red filter at the seashore means a dark gray sky, white clouds, and an almost black sea. Sand becomes ultra light. It's up to the photographer to decide whether this presents a false image of reality or creates a mood in keeping with his film idea. Here, of course we run into the problem of continuity once more. A great many filters obviously cannot be used during a sequence of shots. You decide on a single mood—and stick to it. This, of course, is true for the entire film. It will come out as a better unit if all the exterior shots are treated in the same way.

The addition of a filter over the lens stops part of the light reaching the film and to get the correct exposure the lens diaphragm must be opened up. Correction depends on the fiter and is usually specified by a number. These filter factors correspond to the required increase in lens opening. A factor of two, for example, indicates that the lens must be opened one stop for good exposure. Your original light reading without the filter called for an exposure of

**SHOOTING AGAINST THE LIGHT. —** When used skillfully, this style of photography insures beautiful images with shadows playing the main part. However, you should not succumb too often to the temptation for such effects, since people appear merely as dark silhouettes.     (*Photo by E. Wachsmann*)

f/5.6, so with a filter factor of two you open the lens to f/4. A filter factor of four means two stops more exposure.

Let's take a quick look at some of the filters you may use.

*Neutral density:* This filter has a gray cast to it and it's main purpose is to cut down the amount of light reaching the lens. It has no effect on the gray scale. Neutral density filters come in a variety of strengths and usually are employed when shooting a fast film outdoors in order to prevent overexposure. Also, under certain conditions they can be used to cut down on depth of field.

*Color filters:* They come in a variety of colors—from pale yellow to pale orange, from red to orange to yellow, for example. They are used to achieve varied sky effects, disregarding the rest of the scene. A graduated light filter requires a sliding frame mount and must be placed with extreme care by observing its effect through the finder of the camera. It can't be used for a pan shot if the line of the horizon moves during the take. It won't do for close-ups of people either.

*Ultra-violet filter:* A good bet for high altitude shooting (mountains, airplanes) where haze can be a problem.

*Pola-screen:* Not strictly a filter in the usual sense, the pola-screen or polarizing screen is used primarily for eliminating bad reflections from non-metallic surfaces. It can be used to cut down on reflections when shooting through glass into a street. It also has definite uses when shooting color film. More about that later.

## Use of Light

In one sense at least natural, or sunlight, is more difficult to work with than artificial light. You can't control sunlight—commanding it to stay put. But it does have the advantage of reality and certain technical elements that you can make work for you. Let's look at some of the advantages—and disadvantages—of sunlight.

In shooting an outdoor documentary, the main considerations of light are direction, angle, and height. You make a note of the time of day that the sun comes from the side to make objects in the scene stand out strongly and provides good foreground and background separation.

If you are shooting a scripted film, the problem of relating one shot to another enters. The old devil light matching pops up again. So, before you go ahead and start shooting a sequence that involves several changes of camera to subject angle, you'll also have to check the movement of the sun. If, after a few hours of shooting, shadows begin to change or reshape, you won't have enough time to finish.

If you decide to start your sequence with a long shot to be followed by a series of close-ups, remember to spot your actors so that you'll be able to shoot your close-ups properly.

Clouds are great background devices in a scene. But they too can be tricky and unpredictable. A sudden wind may start them moving right out of the shot. So, before you decide to use clouds in a sequence that requires a great many shots, be fairly sure in your mind that they'll be around for the last of the series.

The sky itself is a great thing for making your shots more effective. For example, including a lot of sky by shooting from a low angle gives your sequences a feeling of spaciousness. But, never place the sky smack in the middle of the frame. Either the ground or the sky can be emphasized, not both. Giving equal treatment results in a rather static, hackneyed kind of composition. There aren't any rules, but a $\frac{1}{3}$ and $\frac{2}{3}$ proportion or visa versa is often employed. Your general approach to framing should be dictated by what the shot has to say—not by arbitrary rules of composition. A foreground that contrasts with the sky provides depth, but conversely, avoid foregrounds that appear too brightly lit. They provide nothing more than a deadly sameness to the overall shot.

Another use of light and shadow techniques: with two people in the shot, one in the foreground, the other slightly farther back, keep one in light shadow, the other in sunlight. This provides a greater feeling of depth to the shot.

Above all, check the position of the sun at the start of a scene. Make sure that it won't duck behind a cloud right in the middle of the take.

## Composition

Long shots of scenery that encompass a wide expanse of scenery are great— providing that they are sharply focused, clearly defined, and not cluttered up with entirely too much detail. But even though the vista is quite lovely, charming, and colorful, don't linger. Movies should move and that means getting back to your actors and the action just as soon as the long shot has made its point. The close-up can match the scenic long shot with only a minor, low key

FRAMING. — There are some cases where the right framing occurs to you right away. But there are places where you hesitate—give it more sky, or more ground, or half and half.

1. This kind of framing gives all the space to the sky. It may be slightly exaggerated although the sky is beautiful. But the village looks like it's hanging in the air.

2. Usually it's a mistake to place the line of the horizon right in the middle of the frame. Here we are with a shot which is something of a mongrel. The cameraman couldn't make up his mind, and the viewer, who cannot do it in his place, feels dissatisfied.

3. This framing, although less appealing than No. 1, is very expressive. The foreground of earth and stone gives the picture a harder, wilder look. The village is featured rather than the sky. The photographer understood this so well that he automatically moves his camera to the right.

(*Photos by Jacques Boulas*)

detail—a leaf, a reflection from a pool, a shadow. If necessary, you can return to the long shot later.

The long shot doesn't have to be a studied type of thing that says, "now look at the scenery." The actors themselves can direct the audience to the background in a natural sort of way. When your actors move, your camera can move with them, showing the landscape in an organic, integrated manner. Camera movement, when it is justified by action, is always more believable. For example, placing people in the front seat of a moving car, with the camera in the rear seat, is enough justification for a dolly shot. It infers that the actors are engrossed in the passing scenery and it's all part of the story. Or, you can pan from a mountain or hill to a valley below by allowing your camera to follow someone walking down the trail. More important, the true size and impressiveness of a structure or natural object in a landscape can be best emphasized by comparison with a man or woman.

Using a second, known dimension to compare with an unknown that must be projected to the audience is a fine device. What can be more explicit than three black dots that are really mountain climbers against a white snow field on the side of a mountain?

### Depth of Field

One of the most effective tools in the hands of the film maker is depth of field—the region in the frame in which objects are apparently sharp. How far this depth of field extends is dependent on lens opening and footage setting. Generally, a smaller diaphragm provides a greater depth of field. However, depth of field diminishes even at small openings when the lens is focused on extremely close objects. Outdoors, in sunlight, you usually can close the lens down considerably—even with filters.

Here's one place that depth of field helps. Suppose you have two or even three characters in a scene. Placing them at different distances from the camera provides an almost three dimensional effect.

However, depth of field also varies with the lens in use at a given focusing distance and f-number. Many lenses have depth of field scales that indicate the distance from the lens to the subject and beyond that the camera is in focus. Or, consult the depth of field table that came with the lens or camera for the exact feet and inches at a particular setting.

Depth of field can be used quite selectively. It's possible, by varying the footage setting to regulate the zone of sharpness. For example, you can throw the background out of focus, keeping only the foreground sharp. Or, the foreground can be unsharp while the background is well defined. Or, both foreground and background to infinity can be sharply in focus.

The wider the angle of the lens the greater will be the depth of field at a given focusing distance and f-number. So, in shooting landscapes you may choose a 17mm wide-angle for 16mm cameras, or a 6.5 for 8mm cameras. However, should you want to cut down depth of field, for an extreme close-up that eliminates all but essentials, for example, you might want a 50mm tele for 16mm work.

Depth of field, combined with other film techniques can produce startling

PORT OF SHADOWS, Marcel Carne (1938). — The very special atmosphere of this film contributed greatly to the fascination it had for the public. The great cameraman Eugene Schufftmann deliberately tried to do away with the depth of field in all close shots. Here, Jean Gabin and Michele Morgan appear isolated. The world around them is reduced to a few shapeless forms and a few shades of grey. *(Photo by Sofradis)*

effects. An overall gray, hazy rendition of fog and rain can be heightened by use of a short depth of field (with a tele perhaps), gray filters, overcast portions of the sky, and background smoke. A variable shutter or neutral density filter makes possible use of wide lens apertures for decreased depth of field.

## When Can You Shoot Outdoors?

With the presently available emulsions, you can shoot at almost any time, in any weather, in almost any light. But, as we mentioned, once you start shooting a sequence in one light, stick to it. Rain, fog, storms, snow, and sun all have their own peculiar beauty. It's up to you to decide how to use it. There are films fast enough to shoot by street light or slow enough to shoot by the most intense sunlight. The use you make of light and film depends on your film making outlook.

CHAPTER 7

# Interiors

The apparently endless possibilities offered for making movies outdoors may be one reason that you've hesitated to move indoors to the rather restricted motion picture making enforced by four walls. For one thing, you're pretty well confined to using interiors as you find them without adapting or changing things to suit your needs.

If you could push back the walls of a particular room it would probably help —but obviously you just can't. So, out comes your shortest focal length lens to make up for the lack of space and to overcome restricted camera movement. This, of course can mean problems, too. Extreme wide angle lenses can mean apparently distorted images if used too close to the main subject or if pans are made carelessly.

## Using the Setting as You Find It

You won't be shooting many long shots indoors. Instead, most of your takes will either be medium shots or close-ups. This isn't quite as bad as you think, because it imposes a rather useful discipline on the movie maker. The human face and its expressions become the important things, instead of large scale action.

Unless you're fairly lucky, your set is going to be your own apartment or home. Actually, almost any room that will allow some camera mobility, that can offer electrical outlets, and that has light colored walls and ceilings should do nicely.

Also, getting permission to use appropriate settings, a store, a work shop, or other set outside the home may be feasible. Tact, an honest approach, and some low key persuasion may swing it for you. Primarily, you'll have to convince the people in charge that you won't disturb routine. You may be able to find the room and materials to reproduce the needed background—but it takes a lot of doing to build a convincing set. Might be a good idea to adjust the story line to what you have available.

Once you've decided on location, other problems crop up—camera location, angle, props. The key to the whole business of contriving a convincing set is simplicity. A few props chosen with care are a lot better than a field of bric-a-brac. Neat lines, simple planes, well defined objects comprise the best kind of setting. The technical problems of lighting a set can be greatly simplified if the setting itself is uncomplicated.

And of course, the amount of light you can command will dictate the speed of

SPOTLIGHT. — The "Spot" directs a precise beam of light on the subject.

FLOODLIGHT. — The "flood," in its reflector, spreads its light over a larger area. *(Photos by Michel Cambazard)*

the film you'll need. Black-and-white films can be exposed at indexes up to 1000 (Kodak Tri-X). On the other hand, a slow, fine grain, panchromatic film may be more in keeping with what you want your film to say. And actually, a minimum amount of lighting equipment makes even the slow films practical for indoor shooting.

## Light Sources

If you film interiors during daylight hours its quite possible to use sunlight or available light as it's often called. However, sunlight does present problems. Unless you use a really fast black-and-white film, characters or subjects will have to be fairly close to the window. And unless you're fortunate enough to have truly huge windows that admit a great deal of light, there's bound to be some fairly dense shadow areas in the room. If you use black-and-white you can, of course, lighten the shadows with artificial lighting.

There are some rather far fetched, and therefore impractical devices for cutting down on the contrast—filters over windows, for example. But their uses are strictly limited.

For most practical purposes, your best bet will be a controllable source of illumination—artificial lighting from photo flood lamps, spots, and the like. But that doesn't mean that you rule out daylight completely. It can be used as a main or even a fill light, supplementing artificial lighting. And there's no reason, even with slow color films, that daylight from a window can't be used if your script calls for it.

But you'll find that regular photographic lights are your best source of illumination for most purposes. They come in a variety of sizes throwing more or less light. Some are of the type with built-in reflectors. Others look like household lamps and require metal reflectors. Be sure not to overload your circuits, two or at the most, three floods at a time are the most an ordinary household circuit can carry without blowing a fuse or tripping a circuit breaker. Spreading the floods around to the various circuits in the house makes it possible for the amateur to bring plenty of light to bear on a scene. Grips and stands of a great variety of designs and shapes make it possible to set the lights almost any place you'd like them. And, you can even place a flood lamp in an ordinary house lamp for natural appearing illumination.

The simplest lighting arrangement requires two or three floods, but the more lights you can use the more you'll be able to control the feeling and appearance of the shot.

Generally speaking, you should first light the background, and then the main subject. One or two lamps are enough for the background. Often, a small room poses the problem of light stands that sneak into the frame. If you can, spot them behind furniture or other props.

Now, for a general lighting plan. The key or main light can be placed near the camera to set the lighting theme for the entire room. Then comes the other lights, the ones that build up faces, clothes, hands, and other important elements in the scene. Actually, floods throw too uniform a light over too wide an area. So, to adequately light small areas you do need adjustable spotlights that concentrate their beams for maximum contrast. One or two 250 or 500-watt

**SPOT USED AS BACKLIGHT. —** A fairly weak spot (250 watts) can add the final touch to the lighting. *(Photo by Michel Cambazard)*

spots can be an invaluable aid if you do a great deal of interior shooting. Incidentally, an accessory outlet box with one lead to the power source and a number of plugs for lamps makes things easier. This is particularly true when lighting the set since many of them have dimmer switches which make it possible to use only half power. This is much more comfortable to work with—especially for your characters if your set is small and liable to get rather warm.

### Light Quality Indoors

I think we've established the fact that the more lights you can bring into a set, the more flexibility you'll have in getting the type of effect you want. Spots, for example, make it possible to create special effects—with faces, shadows, depth, or even shooting against the light. Floods provide the light required for over-all illumination, washing out disturbing shadows, creating an atmosphere of their own.

Good lighting actually has two functions—to provide enough illumination for correct exposure and an interesting atmosphere.

But the most important lighting touch is needed when you shoot close-ups. A book might easily be written on just this part of lighting—but let's just stick to a few simple rules. Above all, avoid effects that overpower the subject—unless you really want to play up the dramatic aspects of a scene through lighting. Strong lighting in one respect should be offset by a softening influence

DIFFERENT TYPES OF LIGHT-ING. — This scene was shot successively with two different types of lighting. This one combines flood lighting in the front, a spot a little to the side on the children and a second spot on the background. The effect of the spot is easily noticeable on the faces, though somewhat softened by the over-all lighting. The light comes from a single direction on to the background and gives an impression of depth.

Here's the same lighting set up, but the spots have been replaced by reflector floods. The scene is now entirely lit by floodlights. Though it's quite satisfactory one can see that the faces are not as well modeled and are less detached from the background, which itself is not as well lit as before.

(*Photos by M. Cambazard*)

SHOOTING AT HOME. — Here's the continuation of the interior sequence begun earlier. "Alice must do her homework, while her brother and her sister are playing, without a care in the world."

**1.** *Medium close-up.* Alice and her mother. The lighting tries to simulate the effect of the table lamp (where a photoflood has replaced the ordinary bulb).

**2.** *Close-up.* "Homework is complicated—and unpleasant." This angle makes for good composition because it frames the subject exactly and contrasts light and dark surfaces. The background is lit softly to intensify the profile of the girl.

**3.** *Medium shot.* Alice in the foreground, the children behind her. Shooting downwards shows the whole scene. However, a large enough depth of field is necessary so that foreground and background are equally sharp. The lens must be stopped down and, therefore, the scene must be lit more strongly.

**4.** *Medium shot* (continued) This type of shot demands a lot of light, perhaps more than we are able to provide, which is why the background is not lit perfectly.

**5.** *Close-up* (*same framing as No. 2*). — The problem can perhaps be solved by inserting close-ups in the scene. The attractions of play are too strong for the little girl who turns and watches enviously.

**6.** *Close-up* (*Shooting downwards*). — The two children at play. Because it's a close-up, this angle is much more eloquent. Since, after editing, this will follow directly after the preceding shot, the action will be perfectly clear, even more so if the editing alternates the two scenes several times.
(*Photos by Michel Cambazard*)

from another direction. For example, if you use a spot to make a close-up of a face stronger, fill in some of the shadows with a flood from the other side.

Avoid extreme angles when setting up your lights for a close-up. There's something particularly ruinous about a light that comes from either an extremely high or low angle. They create almost ghoulish shadows. Fine if your script calls for it—but hardly the thing for a romantic interlude. If you do need the horror effect, you can make it slightly more believable with a flood to fill in some of the shadows. A face can be lit fairly well with a light placed directly in front of it—either at camera level or slightly higher. Or, one light can be placed behind or at a three-quarter angle to the subject for good modeling effect.

Don't make drastic lighting changes from long shot to close-up. As you cut, the light should seem to be the same in both shots. Of course, take advantage of the shadows in one shot to match it to another, if you like—but don't make radical changes that will disorient your audience.

But no matter what the lighting set-up is, good exposure is going to depend on intelligent use of a light meter. If you use a reflected type of light meter, it's best to take readings on many areas of the set, using an average exposure. If you shoot color, contrast ratio should never be higher than three to one.

When shooting close-ups, take your reading directly from the subject—not from the entire set. And above all, make sure that direct light from the floods doesn't hit the meter—or your reading will be way off.

Many professional film makers depend on incident light meters for interior filming, feeling that this type of unit is much more accurate under indoor conditions. It actually measures the intensity of the light falling on the subject—not that reflected from it. It indicates differences in light between darker and lighter areas.

One other thing. Hot spots can be hateful things—particularly when they show up in processed film. Lights from behind or at the side of the set can reflect light in a concentrated form—creating those hot spots. Your eye is the best judge of where they occur. Diffusing cloths over the lights help to eliminate the hot spots. Also, a lens shade indoors is as important as it is outdoors in preventing stray light from ending up as flare on the film. Use them.

## Depth of Field Indoors

No matter how many lights you use indoors, they just won't equal the power of the sun. This means that you'll have to use wider lens openings than in exterior shooting—with a consequent focusing problem. But bringing more light to bear on the scene makes it possible to use smaller lens openings, of course. This doesn't necessarily mean blasting away with a dozen floods, but rather moving the lights closer to the set—keeping in mind the angle of view of your lens.

Chances are that camera and subject will be close enough to make accurate focusing possible by measuring distance with a tape measure. Let's say you have two people seated at a table, one slightly farther away from the camera than the other. Measure both of them for distance from the camera. Then, use a setting, an intermediate one, perhaps, that will give you enough depth of

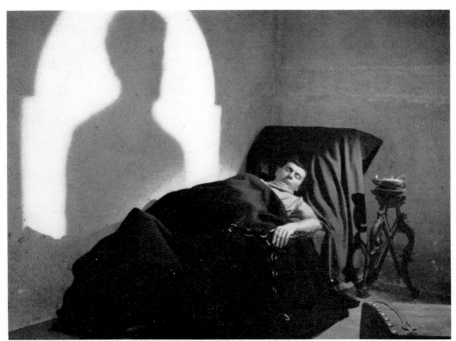

PROJECTED SHADOWS. — In this film about Saint Martin, a shadow suddenly thrown on the wall illustrates the vision of the saint during his sleep. The drawing below shows how the lighting was arranged for this scene. The projected shadow of the silhouette and the archway is obtain by a powerful spotlight. The beam from the spot is sharply defined by the archway and its light touches nothing else in the setting. The other light, justified by the oil lamp, is provided by two back lights and one front light. *(Photos by Georges Régnier)*

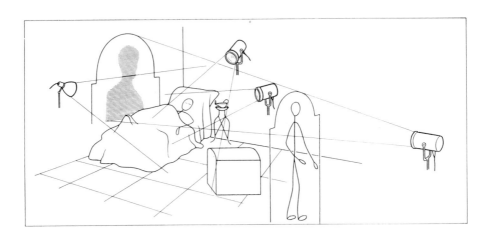

field for sharp images of both subjects.

In some cases you just won't be able to include all subjects within a depth of field at a given lens opening, no matter what the lighting situation. So, here's where some on-the-set editing and directing comes to the rescue. Let's imagine the shot consists of the meeting of three people, but physical requirements of the set demand that they be separated. So, instead of shooting the whole thing at once, you cut from one subject to the other in close-up. Be careful about matching action so that you can splice the shots together without breaks in rhythm.

**Parallax Error**

Parallax is a problem that you run into no matter whether your set is indoors or outdoors anytime you start shooting close-ups. But since you may find yourself shooting more close shots indoors than out, it's something you should pay particular attention to before making the shot.

If your camera has through-the-lens viewing, parallax really isn't a problem. But since most cameras have separate finder systems, you should know something about avoiding chopping heads or leaving out vital parts of the scene. Most finders have some means of parallax correction—good, bad, or indifferent. If yours is the adjustable type, it's important to know the exact distance from lens to subject and to set the finder accordingly. However, if the finder has only indicating marks, you may find them not quite good enough for really close shooting.

Let's look at the problem. The finder and the lens see slightly different things in really close shooting. The slight difference is enough to ruin the shot—unless you compensate for it.

Several methods are available. One, for really extreme close-up filming, is to use a titler as a means for aligning the lens. The head of the subject is framed in the titler frame, with the camera and titler mounted on a tripod. Since the titler automatically lines up the camera, you're all set.

Or, you can use a rackover, if one is available for your camera. Mount camera and rackover on a tripod, sight, move the lens into the position occupied by the viewer, and shoot.

A third method is to use an aligning device of the type that fits over the front of the lens. The Elgeet Cineflex is one such device and for all intents and purposes, turns your camera into one with through-the-lens focusing.

**Preparing an Interior Script**

A shot filmed indoors should be scripted as carefully as one shot on the outside. Let's take use, as an example, a situation that could happen almost anywhere, any place. Our script will take into account the particular problems of interior shooting in conforming to a story line.

Here's the plot. The husband is in his usual hurry to get to work. He shaves while his wife makes breakfast. The doorbell rings announcing the arrival of the mail. The woman takes the mail, looks at it. Among the easily identifiable letters, magazines, and advertisements, there's one letter addressed to her husband. Stationery and handwriting are strange to her. She turns the letter, looks at it from several angles, smells it, and finally hides it.

The husband, rushing, swallows his coffee and burns himself. He looks casually at the mail. The wife looks at him. As soon as he leaves for work, she grabs the letter, tears it open, and discovers that it is nothing more than a subtle bit of advertising with a personal approach.

Here's how the script is prepared from the outline. It's built around one object—the letter—similar to the exterior script built around the flowers.

| | |
|---|---|
| *Fade-in on close-up* | Husband is shaving in the bathroom. He is in a great hurry. |
| *Medium close-up* of the bathroom is visible) | Wife goes by, carrying the tray with the breakfast. She glances toward the bathroom to see how her husband is doing with his shaving. |
| *Medium close-up* of the living room | She places the breakfast on the table and begins to serve. (Ring of the door bell.) |
| *Close-up* | The mail is being slipped under the door. |
| *Medium close-up* (short vertical pan) | Wife picks up the letters and looks at them. |
| *Close-up* | Husband shows his head in the door and asks: "what is there in the mail?" |
| *Medium close-up* (¾ back) | Wife has placed the mail on the table and examines one letter which she cannot identify and which does not bear the name of the sender. |
| *Close-up* | She turns the letter in her fingers, smells it. |
| *Medium close-up* (front) | Finally she slips it under the tablecloth. |
| *Medium close-up* of both | Husband comes in, tying his tie. He sips his coffee, looks at the mail and opens one or two letters. |
| *Close-up* | While buttering a piece of toast, wife watches her husband. "Didn't he expect another letter?" |
| *Medium shot* | Husband replaces his cup, puts on his jacket, grabs his briefcase, hurries toward the door. Wife accompanies him. |
| *Close-up* | At the door, a farewell kiss. |
| *Long shot, zoom in* | Wife comes back to the table quickly, takes |
| *Medium close-up* | the letter and opens it. |
| *Close-up* | Her face brightens. She smiles. |
| *Extreme close-up* | The letter in her hand. It is an advertisement |
| *Fade-out* | skillfully presented as a personal letter. |

There are at least two important elements in the script. One is that just two people can create an interesting situation. If we were to linger over the idea, we could easily develop everything from comedy to tragedy with the two char-

117

MARRIED LIFE. — You can transform your apartment into a studio to meet a variety of cinematic needs.

1. *Medium close-up.* "Coffee's ready!" The lady of the house comes out of the kitchen and crosses the frame. Her gesture and her look while calling her husband lead us into the next scene.

2. *Close-up.* Her husband is shaving. The bathroom lends itself well to the lighting; the light walls act as a screen and reflect the light. Don't forget that to achieve the correct focus of a person seen in a mirror you must add the distance from the subject to the mirror and the distance from the mirror to the camera.

5. *Medium close-up.* "Ah, a letter from Henry . . . a catalogue . . . oh, the telephone bill!" She goes through the mail while walking toward the camera. She goes out of the frame at the left. . .

6. *Close-up.* (shooting slightly downward over her shoulder) . . . and enters the new frame on the right (matching direction). The angle draws attention to the letter she is trying to identify.

**3.** *Medium close-up.* Wife places breakfast on the table. The curtained window makes a pretty background but the front lighting must be well balanced because of this very light surface.

**4.** *Extreme close-up.* The morning's mail has been slipped under the door. This shot would obviously be better if introduced by a sound effect of a doorbell. Notice how this close-up shortens time, because we are now going to see the woman immediately again in the vestibule.

**7.** *Close-up.* "anything interesting in the mail?" This shot must "balance" with the preceding one. The actor is framed somewhat on the left, as the woman was just framed somewhat on the right. The empty portion of the frame should always be in front of the person in the direction of his look.

**8.** *Extreme close-up.* The wife turns over the letter several times "No return address." The meaning of this angle depends entirely upon the playing of the wife.

9. *Extreme close-up. (continued).* She glances in her husband's direction. As she moves her head, she comes slightly closer to the camera. Her look thus takes on more importance.

10. *Medium close-up.* She hides the suspicious letter under the napkin. This shot matches the preceding one and enlarges upon it to show the action. Both these shots could be tied together by a backward dolly shot.

13. *Medium shot* (same setup as in No. 11). The husband swallows his coffee and his mail at the same time. A technical point: the reflection of the flood in the window should have been avoided; usually it's enough in a case like this to open the window slightly to eliminate unwanted reflections.

14. *Medium shot.* Goodbye kiss at the door. Because of the change in place this shot avoids having to match action with the preceding one. Once again it is a shortening of time.

**11.** *Medium shot*—The husband walks in knotting his tie and glancing quickly at the mail. By means of this cut from one person to the other, we have again shortened time.

**12.** *Close-up.* Wife looks at her husband out of the corner of her eye. Shooting downwards slightly we underline the scene by giving direction to her look. Remember to match the hand movements. The same gesture must follow from one shot to the other.

**15.** *Medium close-up.* She comes quickly back to the table, seizes the letter, opens it. This take would lend itself very well to a dolly shot to catch her change of expression while she reads the letter.

**16.** *Close-up.* She smiles, reassured. If this is a cut from the preceding shot, be careful of the matching of hands holding the letter and the envelope. You might also wish to use an extreme close-up of the letter, called an "insert." (Photos by Michel Cambazard)

THE LIGHTING SETUP. — Let's step behind the camera for a moment. Here we see the lighting used for the scene corresponding to photo No. 3. The lighting is simple: three 500-watt spots, two paired floods. Another spot is used for backlighting. The two spots on the side balance the light, one lighting the woman, the other the table. The floods in front counterbalance the daylight.

*(Photos by Michel Cambazard)*

acters in the script.

Second, the script demonstrates the value of simultaneous or parallel action in a film. The action goes from one character to the other, giving it a nicely paced feeling. This can get a bit tired when overdone. Case in point is the gangster film that shows the hoodlums fleeing in one shot, cuts to the chasing police, and cuts back to the hoodlums.

But one advantage in the type of situation shown by our script is the ability to isolate the characters with close-ups. Lighting is easier. The widest shot is a medium close-up, lit by two floods in front and two or three spots for faces and important props in the scene. Daylight might be used to balance the lighting, with artificial light acting as a fill. Floods could be used to lighten shadows and spots to add to the effect of natural backlighting.

This type of script is best played against a simple set—without distracting objects in the background. One detail, a decoration perhaps, is enough to give the feeling of authenticity without distracting from the essentials of the sequence.

What do you need to successfully shoot a sequence? Enough space to perform the actions necessary to telling the story. Enough light to adequately light the set. Enough time to stage, rehearse, light and shoot the sequence. Enough cooperation to do the job without fuss and feathers.

In fact, these requirements just about cover any interior shooting. Line them up and you're on your way to successful indoor movie making.

122

CHAPTER 8

# Color

In the first discussion of color and black-and-white film at the end of the chapter on the role of the producer, I mentioned that color presented certain difficulties not present in working with black-and-white. I also stated that while color is more satisfying to work with, that it might be a good idea to gain experience with black-and-white. But progressing to color doesn't mean giving up black-and-white. They represent different means of expression. Color comes nearer to producing things as we see them and at first glance appears more attractive to the movie maker. However, black-and-white has its uses—representing a perhaps more stylized way of expression. While black-and-white is certainly less pretty than color, it can often be more powerful and more eloquent.

Engraving and drawing, definitely art in terms of gray, has existed alongside of painting for many centuries. While the drawings and etchings of daVinci and Rembrandt don't have the showiness of their paintings, they still have a beauty all their own—perhaps of even greater intensity than the paintings. And as far as motion picture making goes, black-and-white is hardly out of style. Standard screen black-and-white films are very much in evidence because of the ability of the medium to strongly express the emotional qualities of a story.

But color opened up new dimensions to the motion picture. Only color can express the blueness of the water under the surface, or the starkness of desert sand, or the green of a lush field. Color film has made it possible to bring the world of another art—painting—to millions of people.

However, color has its drawbacks in motion pictures. It may be that it takes a bit away from the heart to give it to the eye. Color would have added nothing to Chaplin's tramp, to his bewildered eyebrows, to his sad, sad eyes, to his ridiculous mustache.

On the other hand, color brings fantastic advantages. It provides a rendering of the reality of nature impossible in black-and-white. More important, it provides the illusion of reality. These are the qualities you need for the filming of the personal or family movie and for the travelogue. Without doubt, the introduction of color film has been responsible for the fantastic growth of amateur film making.

Kodachrome, the most widely used color film in the United States, is sharp, practically grainless, and available in both 8 and 16mm. And there is Anscochrome and Super Anscochrome for 16mm filmers. They are faster, somewhat more grainy, and slightly different in color rendition. There are other color films on the way, both from U.S. manufacturers and from abroad.

Color film, while it requires slightly more precise exposure methods than does black-and-white, presents no real difficulties. You may find that color is limited by existing conditions. While the film and the processor does most of the work, there are a few things you'll have to be aware of to shoot successfully. You'll have to watch for extreme ranges of contrast, light direction, matching of colors from shot to shot, and choice of subject and color combinations.

## Color Filming

When you shoot black-and-white, going from an outdoor shooting situation to an indoor one simply means that indoors the film speed will be slower. Not so with color. Other factors enter into the picture. Because of the difference in shooting outdoors and indoors, two types of color films have been developed —daylight and tungsten. The films are balanced to match the different color temperatures of tungsten and sunlight. Using tungsten outdoors, or daylight with artificial lighting without proper correction filters can be disastrous.

*Color temperature:* Different intensities of light produce different radiations of the spectrum under which objects change their color. The English Physicist Kelvin made a study of the modification of the spectral composition of an object under the influence of a given temperature. He invented the unit for measuring light intensity called degrees Kelvin.

Light from the sun has a color temperature (5900K) different from that from a photo flood (3400K). Thus, film designed for daytime sunlight is balanced to account for the greater amount of blue light in sunlight, while tungsten film is balanced for the red in artificial light. Colors are said, incidentally, to be cool when they tend toward blue and warm when they show a reddish tinge. The higher the color temperature, the greater the amount of blue light, and the less there is of red. If you need to use a daylight film under artificial light you'll need a blue filter (Wratten No. 80) while a tungsten (or Type A as Koda-chrome is called) film in daylight requires a red filter (No. 85 or Type A). These filters are generally called conversion filters.

There's a serious loss of film speed in converting daylight to tungsten use— serious enough to make adequate exposure almost impossible even with a battery of lights. However, the loss with Type A or tungsten films isn't serious. One solution to using daylight films indoors is lighting with blue floods.

Here's one thing you may come up against in shooting interiors during daylight hours. Included in the scene of the room (lit by artificial lighting) is a wide expanse of window with lots of daylight pouring through it. The combination of photo floods and natural light is going to be too tough for tungsten film to handle alone. There are at least two solutions.

1. We've already mentioned the first, using daylight film and illuminating the interior with blue floods to match the daylight from the window.

2. Use tungsten film and light with artificial illumination. But take care of the daylight with red plastic filters large enough to cover the entire window area. You can get them at a motion picture supply house or a good camera shop. The filters will block most of the blue light and let the red pass, matching up with the tungsten lighting.

Color temperature vary with sunlight, too. In fact, it changes rather radically

AFRICAN SCENES. — It would be pointless to talk of color with a black and white photograph as an example. Let it suffice to say the cinema would have imperfectly recreated certain aspects of life in Africa particularly, if it had not reproduced that life in color. (*Photo Georges Régnier, taken from the film "Les Paysans Noirs"*)

during early morning and late afternoons in comparison with what it is from about 9:30 a.m. to about 3 p.m. Sunlight also varies according to climate, humidity, atmosphere, time of the year, and geographical location.

The best way to handle color temperature is with a meter designed to measure light in degrees Kelvin. The color temperature meter indicates just how closely light corresponds to the balance of the film and what filters are required to bring them together. Color correction filters (CC) come in red, blue, yellow, and green, either in glass or as gelatins.

If you don't want to get involved with daylight color correction, it might be wise to avoid shooting early or late in the day, when red light dominates— unless you're after a special effect.

On the other hand, large shadow areas under a bright sky, distant mountain ranges on a cloudy day, snow, aerial views, and beach scenes often photograph on the blue side. A CCR (red) filter or Ultra Violet filter can correct for this situation.

Getting back to indoor shooting again, the age of the bulbs you use for your lighting can effect the color, too. Old bulbs naturally tend to burn less intensely than do new ones. Thus, as the temperature decreases, the amount of red light increases. It's a good policy to change bulbs fairly often when shooting color. Save the half-used lights for black-and-white.

## Contrasts and Dominating Colors

Since shooting color requires a lot more attention to the details of exposure, an exposure meter is just about a must for really good results. Of course, many film makers have gotten along quite well with the little slip of exposure instructions that comes with every package of film. But, there are bound to be many situations that depart from the average conditions specified in the instructions.

Color films like Kodachrome, the most popular with amateurs, won't tolerate more than one-half stop over or underexposure. Faster films, such as Kodak Ektachrome Commercial and Anscochrome allow more latitude, but not enough to make serious errors correctable even in the lab. Overexposure means washed out images, while underexposure results in dark pictures that often won't project any detail at all.

The lack of real exposure latitude with slow color films means that unlike black-and-white films, they won't handle extreme ranges of exposure in a single scene—extreme shadows and extreme highlights, for example. Either one or the other is going to be poorly exposed. But even though you should avoid really strong contrasts, that doesn't mean that light should always be flat, coming from behind the camera. Movie makers today realize that provided they avoid deep shadows, side lighting is fine for color—making for sharper looking images compared with front lite scenes. Even more radically, shooting against the light is quite possible with modern day color films.

Quite often, you'll find natural reflectors—water, clouds, brightly lit buildings—work to soften contrast by reflecting light into dense shadows. Even the soft, hazy lighting of an overcast day works to the benefit of color film—unlike the case with black-and-white. The sky acts as a reflector, diffusing the light evenly and providing a soft illumination that works to intensify colors.

Thus, color film can record the feeling of a place that is imparted by light— the transparency of air on a bright, dry day, the remoteness of distant hills on a hazy day, the brightness of green landscape, and the freshness of a newly born spring.

So far we've touched on long shots, but now let's get back to the close-up. First, remember to avoid deep shadows on the face. Just as in black-and-white filming, you may need reflectors to soften shadows. Skin tones in close-ups should be watched carefully. In late afternoon, a person's face may appear to be orange, reacting to the dominance of red light at that time of the day. While that's not necessarily bad if the viewer understands why and when, an unexplained reddish or orange face looks weird on the screen.

Even during good shooting hours, little things can creep in to ruin natural looking skin tones in a close-up. If you shoot on a lawn, the bright green of the grass is quite liable to be reflected into your subject's face, for example. A dark shadow of a wall, for instance, may throw blue light. If you don't want to correct with filters, you may be able to help the shot by showing enough of the surrounding scenery to justify the color shift in the close-up.

Shooting color indoors means primarily working for uniform lighting without shadow spots. The exposure meter should never indicate more than one stop difference between any part of the scene and another.

## Color and the Director

If you look back at what's been said, it may become apparent that the hardest element to control is color matching. You've already heard a great deal about matching—light, action, direction—and you'll hear even more about it in the next chapter on editing. But matching takes a particularly important place in shooting color film. Changes in light modify colors. That means a change in light direction, location, or set from one shot to another may result in a sequence of shots that is rather jolting to put it mildly. So, you have to pay particular attention to the color harmony of a series of related shots making up a sequence. Where the change is a straight cut from one shot to another in a definite change of locale, mood, or action, a dissolve or fade may provide the needed transition.

Because you can control the lighting for interior shots, color matching isn't too much of a problem. It's when you move the camera outdoors that you run into trouble. Absolute control means bringing a great many techniques to bear—color correction with filters, artificial light sources for the shadows, and other devices.

The professional working with negative or a color film designed for making additional prints can have some control through laboratory processes. He can get what is called a timed print, where variations in color can be corrected in an optical printer.

The best way for the amateur is to avoid shooting the various segments of a sequence over a wide period of time. If you can, shoot all the takes on the same day—or just as long as the color quality of the light remains constant. Another bit of insurance—shoot all the scenes for the sequence on the same roll of film—or on film having the same emulsion number. This means that you can at least be certain that any variation from the norm as far as color rendition goes will at least be uniform.

An additional precaution is the avoidance of using too many different shooting angles. If the subject must turn, make sure that he or she doesn't get too far from the original direction of the primary source of light. If the subject must move in front of the camera, be sure that light and shadows aren't extreme.

Above all, watch those backgrounds. If your first shot has a blue sky, you just may have trouble making a harmonious cut if the house in the following shot is pink. In fact, watch your backgrounds throughout a sequence as long as the sequence deals with the same time-space unity in each shot. Naturally, if the setting or background has to change in keeping with the script, don't be afraid to make a really radical change in atmosphere. You can add a dissolve or fade to create the right bridge between shots. But don't depend on optical effects to bail you out of every editing jam. They tend to slow pace, and audiences eventually tire of them. In dissolving one color into another, you'll also have to visualize the effect—it just may not be pleasant at all.

## Color and Composition

Thinking in terms of color is quite natural—even when shooting black-and-white. You may have noticed that a particular color combination you expected to turn out quite well somehow never came off in black-and-white. Actually, you tend to think in colors, despite attempts to think only in terms of gray.

One of the temptations of color filming is to overload each scene with a variety of hues—with a resultant multicolored, loud movie. There are times when red, yellow, and blue will look just terrible. Where you can, control the amount of a particular color so that it doesn't overpower, unless it serves a purpose to do so. There are few, if any color composition rules. Often, museums and galleries can be your best teachers. But from experience, here are a few guides that you may be able to apply to your own film making.

In a scene where you have two complementary colors next to each other, but where one is more dominant (a yellow-orange boat on a green river, or a pale green dress on a red velvet couch), the composition is bound to be pleasing. Rather interesting things can be done with a color contrasted directly against another—a pink dress flush against the background of a green apple tree, for example. In shooting close-ups, limit the number of colors within the tight framing to two or three—flowers against a green background, a bright orange against a deep green.

And remember, the eye can be irritated by having to encompass a great many spots of color. The cameraman has to remember that color is not "read" as quickly as the gray scale in a black-and-white frame.

Speaking of gray, there's an interesting paradox that has to do with gray and shooting color film. Gray should be in color. There are neutral zones of gray that act as bridges for the eye—transporting it subtly through the many changes and mutations that take place in colors. The gray building with the blue sky background is certainly a good color film subject, just as is the tiny spot of green moss growing between gray stones. And have you ever really taken a look at the subtle colors in a rainy street—even though the street appears to be gray? Just let a neon sign flash on and you'll start to see the colors.

The professional will often employ a gray backdrop, and then spot a bright dress, or a brown leather chair, or the tinge in a scarf, to provide the intensity of color.

Color plays an important part in editing and unless the action itself makes certain color demands, you'll have to think about the shot to shot relation of color. Most of the time it will be possible to create color bridges from shot to shot by introducing gradual changes, or even by emphasizing sharp contrasts. Professionals, and of course many serious amateurs, depend on making more than one take of a scene or shot to give them the freedom of choice that they may need later to achieve good color harmony in their films.

CHAPTER 9

# You Are the Editor

We've touched on editing throughout this book—with some definite suggestions which will make the final stage of movie production easier. A good shooting script and an eye for matched action can help immeasurably in editing. Once the film has been shot and processed, you've reached the point where your editing board is the next step.

It's almost impossible to overemphasize the importance of editing. It has been the main road to dramatic expression in motion pictures. Perhaps editing is the main tool for making films an art. Here we can experiment with the placement of images in relation to each other, with imparting pace to a film. Without editing, motion pictures may well have remained a documentary tool—never attaining the status of art—never really communicating.

One of the best illustrations of the tremendous importance and power of editing is the experiment carried out by the Russian director Koulechov. First, he shot a close-up of a famous actor. The man did not resort to any particularly meaningful expressions during the shooting. If he had an expression at all it was one of deep concentration. Koulechov cut the shot into several lengths, inserting them among a variety of other images—a table covered with food, the burial of a child, a beautiful girl. After projecting the film he asked his viewers what they thought. All agreed that the actor reflected the various moods expressed in the scenes intercut with the close-up. He appeared to be watching each shot in turn. His face showed gluttony, sadness, and desire. This is what editing can do.

The Russian motion picture makers have made great use of editing techniques—contributing much to its development.

The total effect of a film is brought about in large part by carefully cutting each shot, so that the motion picture, in much the same way as a literary work becomes a composition of properly balanced long sentences counterpointed by short powerful ones.

Editing links two images so that they appear to be one. Watch a sequence showing a man running from his enemies, reach the top of a cliff, hesitate for a second, and then jump, to emerge from under the water to swim away safely, and you have the impression that it all happened continuously. Actually, the action probably was composed from a sequence of shots put together by the editor to form a unit. Here's what a sequence like that one might look like if broken down:

A. Medium shot: The pursued man stops at the edge of the cliff.
B. Close-up: He looks toward the water, turns to look at his pursuers, hesi-

tates, and jumps.

C. Long shot: A body hurtling toward the water.

D. Close-up: The man emerges from under the water and starts swimming.

So, by breaking down the sequence into its individual shots, we see the miracle accomplished by smooth editing. Even the actual dive could have been performed by someone other than our hero. All that's needed is a man whose general height and weight are the same as the hero's. In the close-up B, only the beginning movements of the act of diving was filmed. Obviously, for close-up D, the actor got into the water in place of his diving double, submerged, and appeared on cue as the cameraman started shooting.

### Selecting the Takes

The first step in editing your film is projecting every foot you shot. Taking detailed notes on each scene helps to cut down on the number of times you'll have to project your original footage before you are thoroughly familiar with every scene. After the first flow has passed, you're quite likely to find that some of your favorite footage is rather disappointing. In fact, you may be terribly disappointed in the entire movie at this point. But that's normal. It would take a monumental egotist to fall in love with footage that's out of order, untimed, and even repetitious.

After you've seen the film you can decide which takes (where one action was shot several times) will be used. You can go right into making a rough cut at this point. But, you may not want to risk working directly on original film. Professionals and serious amateurs often get a work print—either black-and-white or color. Original film is sent to the lab and returned with a rough copy that's just fine for doing all the cutting, splicing, and recutting that goes into preliminary editing.

A rough cut is particularly helpful with complex films—guiding you toward a selection of what is good and elimination of what is bad. And if you have more than one take, the rough cut is a good time to decide which shot you think is best. The rough cut is really a mental type of editing—where many important decisions are made but not transferred to the original—for now. But, don't throw away those outtakes—even when they consist of really short film lengths.

### Shot Matching

While actual viewing of your film on a projector is the best indication of what has to be done in the way of editing, you'll need an editing viewer to actually splice the matched shots.

You can construct a rather crude substitute for an editor—but chances are it won't prove satisfactory. Some movie makers attempt to use a magnifying glass for viewing the individual frames—but at best that's hardly a substitute for a good editor, and at worst a rather inaccurate way of doing things.

An action editor, while it cannot give you a true fps rate as you get from a projector, does show the film in action on a ground glass or lens as you crank the rewinds. Many of them have built-in punches that help you make exact

**MATCHING CUTS.** — While editing, you come up against the problem of matching—movement, direction, gestures, etc., which we've been discussing all along. It's also at the editing stage that the importance of this matching becomes evident, as a mistake here can have drastic consequences.

1. With two lenses of different focal lengths, we have filmed successively two passes of this skier. Laying out the two takes parallel to each other on the editing table, we try to match as much as possible between one take and the other. Here, in the beginning of this turn, is an excellent cut. *(Photos by Robot)*

Same picture as on page 58

2. A good cut depends on matching action, but it must also emphasize the overall rhythm of movement. This is particularly important for these scenes taken from our rowing sequence. *(Photos by Michel Cambazard)*

131

frames for splicing—facilitating splicing of matched shots.

As you recall, we talked about matching close-up and medium shot action frame for frame. With an editor, you can choose the two frames in which the action is identical for the smoothest transition from one shot to the next (as shown in the photographs). The movement starts in one shot and ends in the second.

In examining your footage you may find that there are frames that are definitely unsharp. Splicing the two shots at the unsharp frames provides one of the smoothest transitions possible. Perfect matching isn't easy to find. You may have only one, two, or three frames to work with in each take. It's a good idea to make the cut with a few extra frames at the end of the first shot—and at the beginning of the second one. Later, in the final cutting of the film, you can pare the cut to its precise length and frame. This is a good practice even with work prints and particularly if you work on original film.

## The Cutaway

Naturally, not all the shots in your film follow a matching chain. Only shots involving a particular action match each other. The film story is a resume— a concentrated rendition of the real thing. Only the essentials are recorded and the less important eliminated. However, you must create a continuity between one important action and another. This is made possible by the cutaway.

The cutaway is an interjected detail, an image of some part of the whole scheme of things dealt with by your film that creates a momentary diversion from the main subject. It might be a close-up of some part of an action. The inference is that action itself continues and you can come back to it without it seeming to have stopped at all during the cutaway.

Here's one situation that might illustrate the point. You have several scenes of a wedding ceremony, including the bridal procession gathering as the people emerge from their cars, walking toward the church, going up the stairs and entering the church. It would be impossible to shoot this scene in one continuous run. It probably would be much too long and terribly dull if you could. You actually have the following shots:

—The procession gathering.
—The procession approaching.
—The procession entering the church.

Splicing those three shots alone would provide some rather halting, stammering film. Action would start and then stop, and then start again. Here's where the cutaway comes in.

One cutaway might be of the bride's mother. Another would be the groom. A third might be a tight close-up of the bride's flowers. You cut these in between the gathering of the procession and the approach to the church. You follow the approach shot with a cutaway of the church tower against the sky and a cut to faces of guests as the procession passes. You've respected the continuity of what happened—but also have truly recreated the atmosphere and feeling of what took place.

## Splicing

Modern day splicers—both those using cement and those using Mylar tape—have made joining two ends of films a fairly easy operation. The entire procedure takes only about a minute—including drying time. Your splicer should be carefully checked to see that splices are made precisely on the frame line. Otherwise, the splice will show up on the screen.

Most splicers come with more than adequate instruction sheets but here are two suggestions that may help you get better splices. Don't scrape so hard that you dig into the film base. The idea is to scrape off the emulsion so that the film cement will have a porous surface to which it can adhere. And don't use more cement than necessary. A surprisingly small amount is needed to make a good, strong bond. Too much cement serves only to soften the film base and weaken the film.

## Motion Picture Rhythm

A cut involving matched action almost dictates the frame at which two images will be joined. But the actual length of the shots, and to some extent the order in which you use them, is largely up to your own judgment. A travelogue or personal film allows much more freedom in length of scenes than in the story or documentary film. But, the choice of shots and the length of those shots are the things that provide your film with its rhythm.

Once you've decided on your best takes, put aside repetitious footage, and having decided upon the position of each scene, you can begin the actual composition of your film.

Various factors enter into film composition—and first of all, your own ideas. One sequence may be calm, another made up of brief but numerous images. One shot may be used several times, intercut between other shots—a locomotive, for example. Brief shots quicken pace, while longer ones slow film pace.

As you may recall, in the chapter on the part of the director, we used a rowing sequence to illustrate how an action could be divided into images within space and time. Let's take another look at that sequence—this time from the point of view of the editor dealing with film pace. You know that the intensity of the race grows as it progresses. Both teams will become more tense as they approach the finish line and the closer the race, the more intense is its rhythm.

To recreate the intensifying pace in your film you may first use long shots that last for a considerable screen time. Gradually, you add closer and closer views of the race. The close-ups grow shorter in length as the pace of the action increases.

Your first shots, at the start of the race, are wide-angle lens views of the general scenery surrounding the event—the river, reflections of the sky on water, light colored boats, and other fairly general established shots. You include scenes of the crowd lining the shore, and the judge starting the race.

Now the race takes over the screen as the camera pans along the race course or perhaps shows the position of the boats from slightly in front. The rhythm becomes faster. The shot length decreases. The number of close-ups showing the efforts of the oarsmen increase. Perhaps the tempo of the stroke will provide the rhythm for the sequence of shots. You follow a shot of the rowers with a close-up of the opposing coxswains, cut back to the oars cleaving the water, and then to the prows of the boats as they fight for the lead. A cutaway, briefly shown, brings the faces of the crowd to the screen. It's followed by an extreme close-up of a stop watch. The rhythm of the film becomes even more intense as you cut back to the extreme close-ups of the faces of the oarsmen, back to the oars, to the straining hands, the shouting coxswains, and then to the faces of the crowd.

But you should insert an occasional wider view which shows the relation of the boats to each other. Finally, the boats cross the finish line, and you cut from very tightly framed close-ups to a long shot of the end of the race. Now comes the faces of the winners, the losers, and the crowd.

What we've shown here is that good editing depends to a large extent on the number and diversity of the takes. You must have the latitude to choose from many images in order to create the impression you want. Actually, the tighter the editing, the shorter the takes, and the more individual shots you need.

The contents and quality of the images must also be taken into account in editing. Occasionally, they may even suggest an idea. The fact that footage never seems to emerge just as you envisioned it, has advantages and disadvantages. An effect you may not have looked for may prove to be the bridge for linking two shots. The photographic quality of a shot—its density, direction of movement, rapidity and color quality—enters into the editing of a shot. So, before you make that final splice look at your film from the point of view of discovering hidden meanings and possibilities.

## A Working Method

Good working habits help editing considerably. Orderliness, cleanliness, and proper procedures make editing enjoyable, too. Here's a few ideas that you can apply to your home setup.

First, you'll need a rack to hang individual lengths of film. Professionals employ a film barrel. This is nothing more than a paper barrel with a rack supported by two braces affixed to it. The rack has small straight pins or nails driven through it for hanging film by the sprocket holes. The barrel should be lined with soft, lintless cloth to keep film clean. Or, you can place the rack on a wall. All shots from a particular sequence go on the pins in proper order. Don't let the ends of the film touch the floor. Place clean cloth under the film. If you use the film barrel, you can place a lamp behind the film for easy identification of each shot. Now, you can modify or change the order of the shots according to color composition, movement, or density.

## The Merciless Cut

Unused takes may be hung elsewhere in the room or at the far end of your editing board. This business of relegating costly, but useless film to the discard pile is a tough one. You'll have to be a bit hard with yourself. Even the shots that you do use will require trimming—and that can hurt, too. Sure, it's great stuff—but how many times have you had to sit through beautifully shot footage

EDITING RACK. — Organizing the various pieces of film in one place make things easier. This type of rack, a common accessory in professional editing rooms, is designed for that purpose. It also offers the possibility of storing the outtakes and of finding them easily if the editing has to be modified later.

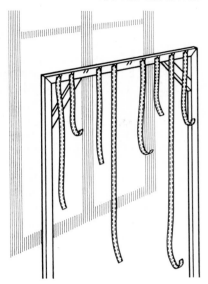

with no more reason for being than it was pretty?

It's too late to cut out footage after a sound track has been added. Some sixty years of motion pictures have provided us with reflexes that almost scream when a shot is too long. An image is immediately identified, understood. It has to justify its existence for every second it spends on the screen.

But if you suffer when you have to throw away "great" footage, so does the professional. The temptation is to keep as much of what was shot as possible. Everything seems essential when in truth a really firm cut here or there can make a great difference in the film's tempo.

Remember, that all those years of going to the movies have provided the viewer with a sophistication that accepts brief images that merely suggest an action rather than elaborate on it. Don't be afraid that people won't understand. Don't burden your film with ponderous transitions. A few well-chosen images can outline an entire action—even a complete episode. It's been said, "Motion pictures are the art of ellipse." It's something to think about.

## Special Effects

Special effects include fades and dissolves (one shot fading in over a shot fading out), wipes, or any means of punctuating the film to indicate the end of a scene or the passage from one scene to the next.

Other special effects which were used so much in the early days of film making are still in use, but not as much as when the camera was looked upon as a "magic box."

George Méliès, great French film maker, had the first idea for special effects in motion pictures. It occurred to him very early in the history of film making. He was shooting a scene from the window of a building on the Place de l'Opera in Paris. Suddenly, the camera stopped working. Méliès discovered the trouble and started shooting again. When he developed the film he found that the camera had stopped working as a bus drove by. When he resumed shooting, he caught a funeral coach traveling in the same direction. In projection, he found the bus magically transformed into a hearse. He immediately saw the possibilities of this kind of optical illusion and the special effect was born.

## Dissolves, Fades, and Wipes

These are the most commonly used special effects.

*The fade:* In a fade-in we start with a completely dark screen and slowly brighten it until the image shows up clearly and sharply. The reverse happens with the fade-out. A fade-in takes place at the beginning of a scene and the fade-out at the end of one. A fade-out is usually followed by a fade-in of another scene.

A fade can be made in the camera by either opening or closing the lens diaphragm slowly. Actually, the correct exposure setting must be rather large for a good lens fade—about f/3.5 or smaller. Diaphragm opening can be increased by using a neutral density filter. When fading out, the diaphragm must be moved at an accelerated pace. You can start closing it slowly, and then increase the speed toward the end of the fade. A fade-in is done in the opposite manner. Smooth fading requires practice.

Some cameras are equipped with variable shutters that can be used to make a fade. Because the variable shutter can be closed completely, results are usually better than with the diaphragm. Some dissolving shutters have automatic features which permit a fade to be made in a specified number of frames. This feature is really great for dissolves, which we'll talk about in a little while.

In the pioneer days of movie making, fades were often made with a special iris diaphragm that fit over the camera lens. The image was made to appear or disappear by widening or narrowing the circular opening of the iris. This is the way that the hopping silhouette of Charlie Chaplin was made to disappear in an ever tightening circle at the end of the film. Since the iris doesn't have to be placed in the exact center of the lens you can fade an image in or out on a given point—a person walking away from the camera, a luminous spot in a landscape, for example. However, the gradual fade possible with the shutter or lens diaphragm is much smoother than an iris fade.

*The dissolve:* This is probably the most widely used optical effect in films— as well as one of the most useful. To make a dissolve, you must be able to wind the film back in the camera to superimpose the second shot over the first. In the dissolve, one scene fades out while the other simultaneously fades in. Here's how to make a dissolve in the camera.

—A fade-out is made at the end of the first shot and the camera stopped. The number of frames of the fade from the start to finish is recorded. A lens cap goes

FADE AND DISSOLVE. — An image "fades to black" by a progressive closing of the lens diaphragm or the shutter. The first series of illustrations shows a fade out on a river scene. Next to it, a fade in on a snow setting. Photographed on the same length of film and carefully superimposed, the fade out and fade in become a dissolve; the snow scene will appear while the river disappears.

*(Photos by Georges Régnier)*

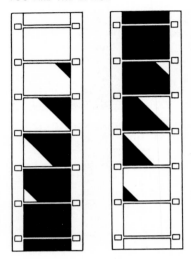

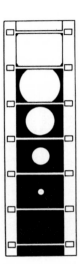

WIPE AND IRIS. — Here are two other ways to make an image appear or disappear. On the left is a sketch of a fade out and a fade in by diagonal wipe. The wipe begins at one corner of the frame and completely blacks it out or uncovers it. These two effects are never superimposed as in the dissolve, but succeed each other. The wipe can also be vertical or lateral. The iris (at right) uses a constantly decreasing circle to end the scene, or an increasingly enlarging one to introduce it.

over the lens.

—The film is wound back in the camera for the exact number of frames of the fade-out. You need an accurate footage and frame counter for best results.

—The lens cap is removed.

—The camera is started again, this time filming the second scene to be faded in. The fade-in is made for the same number of frames that was used for the fade-out.

When the film is processed, the first scene will gradually disappear while the second one gradually appears.

Actually, making a dissolve in the camera isn't the best procedure at all. After you shoot the two scenes, you may decide that they really don't go to-gether—but they are already linked by an unalterable optical effect. Many advanced amateurs and practically all professionals make dissolves and fades in the laboratory—when they are quite sure they want them.

While optical effects are moderately priced for 16mm films, the complexities of optical printing make them rather costly for 8mm footage.

*The wipe:* This is an effect that one is bound to see more often on TV than in a motion picture theater. It's become rather old hat and isn't used by film makers much at all. The effect of a wipe is that of a black screen moving across the image to make it disappear gradually. As the screen moves, it cuts out rather than fades the image. A wipe may come from the side of the image only, or it may have two directions moving toward the center. In some cases it may move from all four sides of the image. Two wipes may be used in opposite directions—one to close a scene, and the other to open the following scene.

Wipes may be made in the camera with the addition of a matte box over the lens. The matte box has channels which permit inserting and moving the wiping mask across the lens field.

When do you use these fades, dissolves, and wipes? It's already been mentioned that they serve as punctuation marks. Two successive fades, one out of a scene and the other into the next, correspond fairly closely to the period and paragraph in written language—or perhaps even to the end of a chapter. Wipes are used in the same way—but usually make less of a division between scenes. The dissolve suggests the passage of time but also serves to link two dissimilar images by creating a unity of thought and feeling.

Optical effects serve to heighten film clarity. They mark the important events and contribute to the establishment of the action. For this very reason they should not be used indiscriminately or just for the sake of showing off filmic virtuosity.

Bad writers are usually noted for their use of exclamation points. Don't overdo punctuation marks in your films. A well planned story can direct attention without using obvious means. I once made a twenty minute film which included constant changes in time and place, and it contained not one fade or dissolve. It in no way impaired the clarity of the story.

## Slow and Fast Motion

Slow and fast motion are often used to heighten the effect of an action—or to minimize it. Normal shooting speed is either 16 fps for silent films and 24 fps for sound. Slow motion means shooting at an increased fps (true slow motion is usually 64 fps, although slower speeds, 32, 48 fps can be used). Film shot at slow motion speeds is still projected at standard speed (16 or 24 fps) and since more frames are used to shoot the action, the effect is slow motion. On the other hand, shooting at 8 fps speeds up action when film is projected at normal speed. Naturally, the diaphragm must be changed—made smaller than for normal speeds at 8 fps and larger at slow motion speeds.

In addition to 64 fps, there are usually other fast speeds on a motion picture camera—and also provision for single frame. Single frame is usually employed for animation work but may also be used for time lapse shooting effects where the speed of a particularly long action can be recorded over a long period of time and compressed into a reasonable screen time—(time lapse of the long process of the budding and opening of a rose, for example).

The various in-between speeds can be used to improve image quality. At 24 or 32 fps (depending at what you normally shoot), unpleasant camera shake, when shooting from a moving vehicle, can be somewhat neutralized. While true slow motion is often used for sports, the intermediate speeds may be applied to such events as track meets, horse races, or even parades.

Shooting at 8 fps can pep up really slow actions—starting of a car, or a slow moving brook. But 8 fps and slower rates of exposure help in poor lighting situations when shooting by available light. The speed permits greater exposure time (at 8 fps most cameras have a shutter speed of about $\frac{1}{15}$ sec.). You must take care that action in this kind of scene is rather slow so as not to appear unnatural. Clouds lazing across the sky can be made to appear to be moving very quickly. The 8 fps speed also has value as a comic device. But it should be used with care. While the jerky movements of people shot at this speed can be laugh provoking, it shouldn't be overdone. The great French film maker Rene Claire used this device very successfully in his early films.

There are other special effects that the movie maker can use to create better films. Let's take a look at some of them.

## Superimposition

The superimposition of one image over another can be used to create a third image. While it often appears to be an artificial cinematic device, it can hardly be called dated. In superimposition, images are registered separately on one length of film either by rewinding the film after the first exposure and adding the second image, or by double printing in a laboratory. Actually, it's quite similar to making an accidental double exposure in a still camera.

In making a double exposure or superimposition on movie film, the second image should be underexposed very slightly. However, it's often perfectly all right to shoot multiple images on one length of film by simply exposing normally for each one. The exposure should be based on the desired effect and experimentation with the images to be superimposed.

Superimposition makes it possible to present a great many images at once to evoke an impression—cars, trains, factories, crowds, musical instruments jumbled on top of each other to present an idea of the sounds of a city, for example. Your own sense of design can dictate the relative size of each image. The musical instrument may occupy one half the frame, and industrial machine appears to cut right through a bus, the crowds may move over the face of the factory.

Superimposition can be used to describe the multiple personalities of an individual. He can be shown walking swiftly down a street and sound asleep on the front porch. We can see him sleeping while his dream self drifts the screen. To make this latter type of superimposition or double exposure, the first image is photographed against a normal background while the second is shot against a bare background. The dream personality can be made to walk through chairs, tables, even walls. For best results, camera position should be fixed while the background changer. A blank backdrop can be placed over the scene for the second shot.

I can still recall the tremendous impression when I first saw superimposition used in a film made in 1920—"La Charrette Fantome" by Sjorstrom. The shadow of a dead body gets up from its funeral bed, while through the hazy-looking walls of the room the funeral coach makes its appearance.

The superimposition can be used to dramatize a thought or obsession. It might be that you want someone to appear in the thoughts and mind of a second person. The first image is photographed normally, while the vision is shot against a black background so as to appear strongly in the finished sequence. This type of thing is rather romantic—and outmoded by current standards because of its over eloquence.

Superimposition is a fine creative tool in the hand of an imaginative movie maker. But a lot of thought should go into its use. Superimposition can solve sticky problems that might otherwise cost a fortune to overcome.

Several years ago I had to shoot an electrical storm. Getting anything at all on film during an actual storm would require more luck than any cameraman can expect. More than that, the storm itself would have to be truly dramatic to have real photographic value. And lastly, the amount of film that would have to be wasted adds up to a fantastic figure. This is how we did it.

First, we shot some footage of a landscape under a stormy looking sky. The film was wound back in the camera after a few feet at the end of the take was sent to the lab for processing. The undeveloped part of the film was removed from the camera and marked so that it could be replaced back in the camera without trouble.

Once back at the studio we cut out a lightning shape in the middle of a black cardboard. Behind the lightning went transparent paper and behind that went a second black background.

A frame of the developed film was placed over the lens aperture (after removing the lens) and the lightning lined up on it with the camera's through-the-lens focusing system. The exposed but undeveloped film was replaced in the camera. The camera was started, spotlight turned on for a fraction of a second and directed at the lightning cutout. The surrounding black area had no effect on the film but the impression of lightning registered over the original landscape.

Incidentally, a very long lap dissolve, while not strictly speaking the kind of superimposition we've been talking about, can be used to express a fixed idea in someone's mind. This was used in the movie version of Theodore Dreiser's *American Tragedy* called "A Place in the Sun." A young man attempts to escape from his rather low station into a better one, but is obsessed by a crime he committed. The feeling of desperation is emphasized by extremely long dissolves.

## Reverse Motion

Reverse motion is not necessarily restricted to the type of shot that shows a diver who emerges feet first from the water and lands back on the high board. Reverse motion can be used to recreate an automobile accident, an acrobatic stunt, a knockout punch, or any other dangerous motion.

The movement is made in reverse, the camera held upside down and the footage exposed. The processed film is turned around end to end during editing. With 8mm, the film must also be turned over or recopied so that refocusing won't be necessary during projection since the emulsion position is changed. The effect is usually coupled with 8 fps shooting.

Let's see how the automobile accident sequence is made. The cars are supposed to collide. Instead of starting out with the cars at opposite ends of the roadway, we place them bumper to bumper. Unless you can shoot in reverse (as with an Arriflex) turn your camera upside down and set it at 8 fps. Start shooting, and have the drivers of both cars go in reverse. After turning the film end for end it will appear as if both drivers hurtled toward each other at tremendous speed. Cut the film at the impact point when editing, and insert several close-ups—the drivers' faces, the moving wheel, the locked bumpers, a person's head against the windshield. If you use sound effects the shot will be more convincing.

I mentioned that difficult acrobatics can be made easy with reverse motion. Suppose you want to shoot a sequence showing someone climbing up a rocky cliff. During the climb he leaps up and grasps the overhanging branch of a tree, pulling himself up in one smooth motion. Shoot the scene in reverse, with your man letting himself down from the tree with his arms extended. When you reverse the picture it will look as if he made a graceful leap and grab at the limb, and pulled himself smoothly up. We made this kind of shot several years ago, and it looked fine—until someone noticed that the pipe our young man had in his pocket had slipped out during the take. Thus, when we reversed the film we found the pipe had made the leap with the actor, following him up gracefully and landing conveniently back in his pocket. You'll have to check details like that—and also make sure that there's nothing in the background that will give the shot away.

## Diffusors

Today, we want sharpness in our film images. We go to great lengths to achieve overall sharpness on a wide field. But it wasn't always that way. In the thirties, the tendency was toward hazy images, diffused lighting, and general softness. It was considered quite artistic. The fashion just might make a come-back someday. To obtain these effects, diffusors made of lined glass or thin fabric were used, sometimes placed close to the lens to cover the whole frame, or to simply diffuse the outer edges of the image, but leaving the central part of the scene sharp. In the latter case a piece of muslin placed in a wood frame was held at a distance from the lens. A hole was cut in the middle of the muslin for the central image to register sharply.

While the diffusor has its uses as an evoker of things past—by making a scene appear to be a hazy recollection—there are more original uses. A recent Japanese film called "The Wild Flower" makes just that use of diffusors—making all scenes that are supposed to have taken place in the past appear hazy. But diffusors can be used to change the shape, lighting, or meaning of an image. Emphasis can be placed on a scene showing morning mist, or the sky-line of a city can be given a fairyland feeling.

There are graduated diffusors, by the way, that are used to transform clear skies into dark foreboding ones with a progression of shadings that go from the horizon to the top of the frame.

## Prisms

A many faceted prism placed in front of your lens will multiply the same image several times. If the prism is put into motion the image will appear to turn. Hollywood uses this system to put over the idea of the groggy fighter or the man seeing double after too many drinks.

But other effects are possible with prisms. You can lengthen or shorten a line for comic effect in the way the funny mirrors in an amusement park distorts images. Orson Wells, in the filming of "The Lady from Shanghai," used prisms for that type of effect. But prisms have been used by serious film makers to achieve new images. H. Francis Thompson, in "N.Y., N.Y." used prisms to express the fantastic rhythm of the city.

But image distortion can be accomplished in other ways, too. The film maker can throw things out of focus, film rising heat waves with a telephoto lens, or

THE USE OF MASKS. — These two young-sters are actually the same child. The left half of the frame was blocked by a mask and the child was photographed in the right half (obviously, his hand could never pass the center of the table). The film was rewound in the camera and the mask was moved over to film the child this time in the left half of the frame.

(*Photos by Jacques Boulas*)

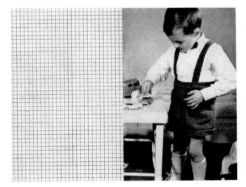

slip a vaseline covered glass over the lens. In one sequence I can recall, glycerine placed at the top of a piece of glass ran down slowly to create a gradually blurred image expressing the feeling of a woman's eyes slowly filling with tears.

## Masks

The mask, as its name implies, is something which covers a portion of the frame. In the old days of film making, they were used to give the impression of looking through binoculars or a keyhole. While they were great stuff in the silent days, you don't see much of it anymore. Occasionally, you may see a split frame effect. Two separate images occupy the frame, each taking half the screen. Here's how it's done.

A matte box is mounted on the lens. Then a mask is slipped into the box about half way so that only one half the lens receives any light. The shot is made. It might be one of your son sleeping. The film is rewound, the mask moved to the other side of the lens, still only covering half of it. You might shoot the boy playing with his dog this time. Often, actors are shot doing two diametrically opposed things—playing tennis and skiing. In fact, it was used in a recent Fernandel film, "The Sheep Has Five Legs." In the shot, there are six Fernandels. Of course, for a successful shot, the action must be carefully planned, and exact marking of the field of view of the lens, and severe limitations put on the actor's movements. And of course, all the shots can be made normally and then combined on the same frame in the lab. But it can be rather expensive.

## Stop Motion

In a previous section in this chapter we mentioned the accidental effect achieved by Méliès—the sudden substitution of the funeral coach of the bus. While this is one of the more spectacular of the various special effects, it's one of the easiest to create. With the camera firmly mounted on a tripod you can, by first stopping the camera, then starting it again, modify one or several elements in a scene—without destroying continuity. You've probably seen films where a man reaches out into thin air and grabs a cigarette. You can make pieces of furniture appear one by one in an apparently empty room. A character can materialize in what was a second before just empty space.

Here's how it's done. Let's take the case of the man who magically takes a cigarette from space. The camera starts and the man reaches out his hand. He stops his hand motion but keeps it in precisely the same position. A cigarette is placed in his hand. Once he has it the camera continues to film. Furniture can be made to appear in the same way. You shoot the empty room, stop the camera, move in a chair, and start shooting again. Repeat the procedure until the whole room is decorated. Things can be made to disappear by reversing the procedure —that is, stopping the camera and removing the object before running the camera again.

The key to stop motion success is to have either inanimate objects or people with a great deal of self control in the shot. Any change in position will be registered on the film—and ruin the effect.

## Titles and Subtitles

Your main concern will be with main titles and credits rather than subtitles —which have more or less passed by the board even in amateur films. In fact, many, many amateurs are adding live sound to their films, making any type of subtitle superfluous. Even when viewing old silent films that depended on sub-titles to carry what little dialogue was needed to tell the story, most movie audiences are sophisticated enough in cinematic techniques not to need them. The white letters that flash across the screen with such informative bits as "Marguerite had not guessed that Leo loved her secretly", or "the driver liked hot dogs" seem gauche.

So, let's talk about titles in the main. If you do use subtitles they'll simply be place or time designations—simply worded and spread sparcely through the film.

One of the more annoying habits of the professional film makers is the subjection of the audience to a seemingly endless string of titles, credits, and what have you. There are times when you aren't too sure that the man who operates the studio commissary isn't in the credit list.

A film starts with its first image—the title. The title creates a mood—and because it does, it is an integral part of the film. For example, letter style has a lot to do with the way people feel about a film. A design employing a gay nineties type of script puts them in one mood. A title with rather modern, bright letters has another effect. A title superimposed over action has still a different feeling.

You can have your titles made in a laboratory—where they'll do all the work from designing to lettering to shooting. Or you can make your own titles. The basic requirements for making good titles at home are patience, imagination, and accuracy.

One of the first, and incidentally easily solved, problems in making the titles is framing the title so that it will be accurately aligned with the lens of your camera. There are a number of titling machines built along the lines of an optical bench on the market. Practically all of them have some kind of device for automatically aligning the camera lens with an easel that holds the title. Most of these titlers can be used in either horizontal or vertical position. Acessories make all sorts of titles possible—flip flops, roller, traveling, etc.—with a minimum amount of technical difficulty.

Title lighting can be as simple as placing two floods on each side of the title so that light distribution is even. The simplest way to create a title is to use the standard letters that come with the machine. However, there's no reason why you can't use poster paint to create your own original letter designs. Often, a cel (cellulose sheet) is used as a title carrier. Letters are either painted or printed (via a hot press) on the cel and the cel overlaid on a black back-ground or special background photograph, non-objective design, or painting. Simply placing black letters on a white background is rarely the most successful type of title. The letters look unsharp and the white background tends to be annoying. You can use stop motion or animations to make interesting titles. One way to do it is to place the camera upside down, line up the title and

145

shoot about a foot of film. Then, remove the last letter and shoot one frame. Remove the next to last letter and shoot another frame, and so on until the title is completely removed. When you flip the film end for end (and turn it over in the case of 8mm), the title will appear to jump into place one letter at a time until all the words are spelled out.

If you follow your title with a list of credits, a short fade or dissolve should be employed to link them together smoothly.

### Superimposed Titles

In professional films you often see the title fade-in along with the opening scene. This is probably one of the best ways to establish the atmosphere of a film. The action combines with words to set a definite mood.

The superimposed title is certainly within the powers of the amateur film maker. There are two ways open to him—have the laboratory do it or shoot the superimposed title right in the camera.

In the first way—with the lab—the complete film is photographed and edited. Then, the title is shot. Usually, the title consists of white letters on a jet black background. You shoot the title on black-and-white film (even though your film may be in color) and send both the opening scene and the title to the laboratory. Usually, the title can be added most easily if and when you duplicate the original film. However, if you desire, the lab can duplicate only the sequence to carry the title. Each lab has its own specific requirements as to instructions to the printer. Best thing to do is check with the lab before shooting the title. The actual duplicate from your title and original is then made in an optical printer. Some labs will take your copy and shoot the title for you. It all depends on what you want and how much you can spend.

If you decide to make the title in the camera here's the procedure you should follow. Set up your title on a black background. White letters provide the best results whether shooting with color or black-and-white. Shoot your title and credits at the start of the roll of film. Note at which point on the footage and frame counter that you finished shooting and then rewind the film to the start. Now, shoot your opening scene exposing as you would normally.

There's one other way to shoot titles on film after the film has been processed —back projection. First, rewind your film so that the emulsion is reversed. Now, place your title letters on a ground glass, line up your camera on one side and the projector on the other. Project the film and shoot it from the other side of the ground glass. Focusing, of course, should be on the camera side of the glass. At best, unless you have some way of synchronizing camera and projector the results will be crude.

Other titling ideas will occur to you as you shoot your film. It's almost a cinch that if you see a beach film you'll also see a title written in sand—with the waves washing it out. Seek the original—but within limits. Don't let your titling become more important than film making. Fancy scroll letters may be fine for the type of film dealing with a historical idea, but straight modern design is probably best for the majority of titles. Animated techniques with artist's paint brushes, painting one part of the letter at a time, a book that flips

EUROPEAN
NOTEBOOK

**SUPERIMPOSED TITLES.** — Choose a scene which characterizes the style of your film to be used as background for the title. It should be low-key in mood (even if you have to underexpose slightly) so that the letters of the title can be easily read.          (*Photo by Georges Régnier*)

open to the title, then to the credit are all good devices. Even street signs make good titles.

Here's one idea you may want to use for marine films. First shoot the titles on transparency film (color or black-and-white). The 4 x 5 size is easiest to work with, although 35mm will do. Place the slides in a glass bucket or tank of water and light from underneath. The camera is positioned above the titles. Position the lights out of camera range. When you've finished shooting one title blow air across the water with an electric fan for a dissolve effect. Then substitute the next title. Before shooting blow air across the water. Start shooting, cut the air and let the water settle.

The professional film is a good source of titling ideas—the Robert Aldrich film, "The Big Knife," has titles that almost cut right through the screen.

CHAPTER 10

# You Are the Sound Technician

If you think about it, there's really no such thing as a silent movie—not even at home. Even if your films don't have sound tracks, you still supply the narration while watching it. And in truth, there's a certain genuineness in this kind of off hand comment that can be refreshing.

### The Live Narration

Let's suppose you've filmed a travel movie. You don't have a sound track on the film—but still feel that some comment is needed to supply continuity or to elaborate on some of the scenes. You could easily show the film and say the first thing that came into your head. Chances are that it would be quite acceptable. But, as with all impromptu speeches, sentences tend to be a bit long, sometimes awkward, and often unclear. A better way would be to write down some complete thoughts for the spots in the film where you wish to make comments. Keep the sentences short and to the point. Remember, all you want to do is supplement the pictures—not replace them.

After a few showings you'll know your film and script by heart and be able to dispense with the written comments. A few main headlines will be all you'll need to cue you in. This way you'll be able to inject a feeling of spontaneity into your film.

I can recall hearing the first narration for the film that Marcel Ichac and one of his comrades had made for the Annapurna expedition. The narration was exciting and emotionally appealing. Later, I saw the film again in 35mm and with a sound track. The narration had been recorded against a musical background. The film remained a superb one—but the narration, despite its smoothness, had lost some of its feeling of presence, warmth, and emotion. It had become slightly mechanical—almost static. The live narration—with all its faults, hesitations, and improvisations—was more effective.

But the case of Annapurna is the exception. If your film is destined for a wide audience or for many showings, you should consider adding a sound track, either with narration or music, or both. And the doing may not be as difficult as you think.

### The Tape Recorder

A few years ago about the only way that an amateur could add sound to his films without resorting to professional techniques (and a lot of money), was with a double turn table for music and a microphone setup for narration. He rarely saw his own film—since he was fairly well occupied with following a cue sheet and going from one record to the other. He resembled nothing so much as a one man band act—trying to conduct as well as play five instruments.

But tape recorders have changed all that. First, they represent an inexpensive way of recording sound. Second, the recording may be played back as soon as it's made. Third, magnetic tape may be cut and spliced easily. Fourth, the sound quality, even on low priced recorders, is better than what the professional had to be content with several years ago. Practically all amateur sound tracks are recorded after the film has been processed and edited. Here's what a typical setup for post narration looks like.

The projector is placed far enough away from the tape recorder microphone so as not to ruin the track. If possible, the projector should be placed in another room. If there is a glass door which you can project through—so much the better. You have the script prepared, and the background music record on a turntable plugged into the tape recorder. If your tape machine can handle two channels at once you won't need a sound mixer. If not, and you want to record both voice and music at the same time you will need a mixer. They can be had as inexpensively as three or four dollars or for as much as thirty to sixty dollars. If you don't have a mixer, you can first record the music, place a piece of paper between the erase head of the recorder and the tape, and then add the voice. The latter is at best a crude way of doing it.

The usual way of recording the track is to project the film and read the script into the mike—following prepared cues. Most important thing is to see that extraneous noise doesn't interfere with recording. Beware of furnaces going on, people walking in by accident, and even passing automobiles. Select a recording time when you can expect a minimum of interference.

The major problem in tape recorded sound tracks is keeping tape and projector in synchronization. The simplest, but by no means the best, is to use Revere Synchro Tape—a regular magnetic tape that has a strobe effect on its back. Several manufacturers have developed electronic and mechanical synchronizers to keep projector and tape in sync—Bauer, Bolex, and Eumig, among others.

## Magnetic Striping on Film

One of the best solutions to the sound track problem is the magnetic striping on film. The ironoxide coating, quite similar to that used for tape recorders, is

MIXING THE SOUND. — This sketch shows how to achieve the mixing of a spoken narration with background music in the simplest manner, but unless you have a record player with two turntables, you won't be able to dissolve from one musical theme into another. Recording the music beforehand on magnetic tape and playing this recording back with the live narration to be recorded by a second tape machine is a more flexible process.

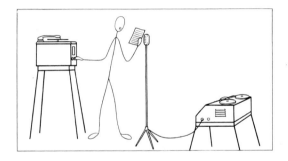

added to the film after it has been processed. Several 16mm projectors—Kodak Pageant, Bell & Howell 302, RCA, and Victor—are made to both record the sound and show and play back. The system works much like a tape recorder. Most of these projectors have provision for recording sound and voice simultaneously. Several 8mm models are in the offing. They are already available in Europe and should be available in the U.S. soon.

## Music and Narration

With the many, many recordings available today, your choice of music for your films is limited only by your own taste and what is most appropriate for your film. Music should be chosen on the basis of the mood which you wish it to impart to your audience. You can even record music off the air on your tape recorder without loss of quality. As long as the film is an amateur one, and not used to make a profit, you don't have to worry about copyright. However, there are recordings for which the copyright has been cleared that you may use for professional films. Several organizations specialize in the distribution of these recordings.

In going from one theme to another (where mood changes and so does the musical selection) you'll have to create a smooth bridge. One way is to dissolve the two into each other—(by mixing and fading one selection in while the other fades out). Or simply fade one out and the other in—providing the mood and pace are not radically different from each other.

As for narration, there are only a few simple rules that you'll probably discover for yourself. Of course, wordy narrations are a bore. Use only the nec-

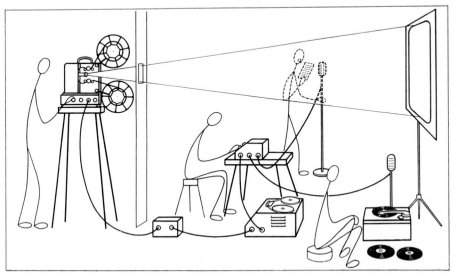

POST-RECORDING. — The film is projected from an improvised booth which deadens the sound of the projector. The "sound engineer" is in charge of the faders on the mixing console. The tape recorder (synchronized with the projector) records the music (carefully prepared in advance to fit the film) and the narration read in front of the microphone.

THE WORLD OF UTRILLO. — (Georges Régnier, 1954) The painter recreated on canvas the image of a long-vanished past. Here is a scene so eloquent that no narration was needed. The narration was designed to just "guide" the emotion of the audience. (*Photo by Georges Régnier*)

essary words. Sentences should be short, clear, and when appropriate—breezy. Avoid lyricism. Remember to allow yourself enough time to breathe between passages. Build your sentences so that they create a rhythm, a tempo which keeps pace with the film. And remember, if you use a tape sound track, don't try to crowd the beginning and ending of a sequence to the limit. Leave enough room at either end to compensate for any failure in synchronization. Overlapping music isn't terribly bad in most cases—but words that don't apply can be funny—when you may not be looking for humor.

Here's part of the narration used for a film on Maurice Utrillo shot a few months before the painter's death. Note the indications for image, music (composed by Maurice Jarre), and narration. This is the track at the end of the film.

The narration for the Utrillo film is a complement to the image—making it more meaningful. It does not try to explain the image since the picture is there and sound cannot enhance it. On the contrary, an intruding sound track can be unpleasant. The idea of a sound track is to emphasize a fleeting impression, or perhaps to supply an explanation the film cannot give with images alone. Be brief, be simple. Above all, don't assume the role of a Shakespearian actor. Speak as you naturally would, keeping your voice under tight control. Since you are speaking into a microphone you don't have to project. Don't shout and don't allow your voice to fall away at the end of a sentence.

| PICTURE | MUSIC | NARRATION |
|---|---|---|
| The studio of Lucie Valore, the wife of the artist. She is painting. The setting around her is composed of flowers, birds, paintings. There is a portrait of Utrillo by Lucie Valore. | The music is a little too sweet. From it will surge, as a strong contrast, the music of the last sequence. | Lucie Valore has brought tenderness and firmness in the life of Utrillo. She has created around him a new universe, stable, concrete and orderly. |
| The studio of Utrillo. The artist is before a painting which he is completing. It represents a street in Montmartre with the Sacré Coeur in the background. | Same theme as was heard earlier in the film, evoking the solitude of the artist. | This is his apparent universe. The other one, the universe made of grey tumbling walls, of weak street lights, Utrillo carries within himself and finds it every night in his studio. This magic universe exists only for him. No one can penetrate its secret or meet |
| A pan discovers the portrait of the mother of the painter (Suzanne Valadon) as well as a few views of Montmartre and some religious objects. | The theme is transformed into a chorale of wind instruments. | him there. This is a closed world, a chapel where the mother of the painter watches over like the figure of a stained glass window. Here is a memory next to other memories. Here is the naive prayer of a simple soul. But the most beauti- |
| Again the painter at work. He stops to light a cigarette, then goes back to his brush. Close-up of his face, of his hand, of the brush, of the touch of paint on the canvas. Slow zooms in on the canvas until it goes out of focus. | The theme expressing not the man but the artist fades in and increases to the end. | ful prayer sings with complete freshness and purity in the brush of the artist. Every touch of his brush is one more step he takes away from us, in the endless street where he often meets the pale silhouette of an unhappy genius: Utrillo. |

## Lip Synchronization

It's strange—but all the problems that faced the professional in making "talkies" in the early 30's, now face the amateur—muffling the sound of the camera, keeping lip movement and sound together, the editing of sound, and the mixing of several sounds.

None of these problems are easy for the amateur to solve—and some of them are downright expensive. There are devices which sync camera and tape recorder—but they run as high as $1500. A few cheaper devices have been developed, but require custom work on camera and projector. You cannot show your films on projectors that have not been specially altered. One such system is added by Synchro-Sound, Flushing, New York. A more expensive unit—the Rangertone—is almost exclusively designed for professionals but there's no reason why the amateur who has the money to spend can't use it.

Professional practice for keeping sound and image together also employs a device called the clap stick. As the recorder and camera begin to operate, an assistant moves into the finder, claps two hinged boards together, announces the take number and other information, and moves out of line. The clap sound is recorded on the tape machine and also on the film. They represent a starting point, and to bring both film and sound into sync, the clap sound and picture are brought together. If a sync system has been used, the two will stay together.

Another problem is keeping camera noise from penetrating the sound track. Professionals blimp the camera—that is, house it in a sound proof box affair that allows controls to be operated externally.

Incidentally, all cameras used for sound filming have synchronous motors that deliver almost exactly 24 fps.

Editing sound film provides additional difficulties. Cuts in both sound and picture must match each other. Sound editing constitutes an art in itself and involves using a Moviola—an editing viewer that also plays back the track. Some sound playback devices have been designed to work with regular editing viewers.

Probably the most expensive aspect of lip sync shooting is the eventual conversion of the ¼-in. tape into 16mm magnetic film and finally to an optical sound track. If lip sync is for you it might be a good idea to contact the Society of Motion Picture and Television Engineers, New York City, for their resources of technical information.

One way for the amateur to record lip sync is to use a single system camera (around $600, depending on lenses and other equipment). This type of unit—the Auricon, for example—records sound and image at the same time. However, the system poses its own peculiar problems in that track and film image cannot be edited separately.

CHAPTER 11

# You Are the Projectionist

This chapter almost brings us full circle. The amateur seems to be everything from producer to property man—and in the final analysis he's also the man who projects the film. And perhaps this is the way it should be. A disinterested party may not be the best person to project—or protect—your film. Quite often, professional films suffer from poor projection techniques. You've probably witnessed instances of improper focusing and poor projection lamps that burned out just at the wrong moment. Sometimes the projector lamp isn't bright enough.

The things to aim for in home projection are bright screen images, sharp focus, and good sound reproduction. The first requirement is a good, rigidly supported screen. Beaded screens reflect more light than matte surface screens. On the other hand, a matte screen reflects an image which doesn't appear distorted to viewers on the extreme sides of the room.

It's a good idea to always have an extra projection lamp and even a sound lamp around, just in case the ones in the projector burn out. Many projectors will take a higher wattage bulb than the one with which they are equipped. Check with the manufacturer for the maximum rating. Check the centering of the lamp in relation to reflectors and condensers. Keep all surfaces clean.

### Setting Up

Arrange chairs so that your audience will be midway between projector and screen. This way, they won't be too close to the image nor far enough back to be irritated by the projector noise. If you find that your room is too small for an adequate image size, use a wide angle projector lens (¾ in. for 8mm and 1½ in. for 16mm films). Focus the projector before the audience is seated and have the first frame of the film in the gate so that all you have to do is throw the starter switch for the film to start.

One other thing. Make sure leaders and trailers are long enough to protect your film. A trailer (piece of leader film at the end of the movie) prevents scratching.

Finally, store your films in a room that is neither humid nor overly dry. Both conditions can hurt film. And keep your films in metal cans that can be tightly closed when the movie is being stored.

CHAPTER 12

# The Scope of Amateur Film Making

It's virtually impossible to place a limit on the amateur film. The area which one finds amateurs at work is getting bigger all the time. In some cases you even see amateurs making films about subjects that were once the property of the professional. And amateurs are forever exploring new fields with their cameras. Scientists, whose film making category can rightly be called amateur, have developed their technique to the extent that one often wonders if they are scientists first or film makers first.

The light 16mm or even 8mm camera has steadily taken the place of bulky 35mm professional film in documentary work, for producing instructional films, and for even advertising and demonstration-type films.

Only 16mm, for example, was adequate for the task of recording the climbing of Mt. Everest and Annapurna, or for documenting the voyage of the raft Kon Tiki. Even 8mm film is finding its way into hospital operating rooms as films, lenses, and cameras become more versatile. Small format film is used by biologists, medical photographers and even X-ray technicians (who incidentally are developing a whole new field). Amateur film making may perhaps be the wrong term for what non-professional film makers and those who use 16mm or 8mm as part of their work, are really doing.

If you look at your own way of making a living you just may find an application for motion pictures that will improve a product, an approach, a technique. Certainly, films constitute one of the most important sales techniques.

## An Occupation Film

Even if you have no desire to make a film for business reasons, you may find that what you do for a living can provide wonderful material for film making. If you take a really close look you may see things that have tremendous photographic possibilities—the people who you work with, the shape of the buildings, the way the sun comes through the windows, or small symbols that exist in every office.

Besides, you know your office, or factory, or farm. Therefore, it follows that you have one of the most important assets in telling a film story—familiarity with the subject. You understand the interrelationship of people with people, people with job. If you take a look at professional films, you'll quickly recognize that the character of a particular social group is put over by accenting gestures, language, clothing, traditions, and humor which typify it.

Your group can serve as the starting point of a story—rather than the story itself. The general background may be all you'll need. If you own a store or

**THE NATURE FILM.** — The motion picture plays its most noble role as an instrument of education. We rarely forget the images of nature which we see in movies because they represent life itself in all its grandeur, its power, its necessary cruelty. In this quest for documentary truth the small format motion picture leads the way. (*Photos taken from "The Living Desert" and "The Wide Prairie," Walt Disney Productions*)

**THE INDUSTRIAL FILM.** — Utilitarian and functional forms can be photogenic, too. This ammonium storage sphere is just one example among many. The dynamism of motion pictures goes well with the rhythms of modern industry. The small format allows the engineer to become his own film producer. *(Photo by Georges Régnier)*

other establishment where people come and go all day you may have a ready-made script right at hand. The different faces and personalities are a story in themselves. People look through the display windows, at the counters, through the door. You shoot them inside and outside the store. Instead of a documentary type of film, you'd rather work out a fiction idea. Recall the things that have happened in your store—the irate customer, the attempted petty theft, the timid soul who didn't want to make a decision.

The engineer or industrial worker has a story to tell—and film may be the best way to explain what he does for a living. This is the film that can be shot when its subject is actually happening. If you work on huge construction jobs—building a dam or constructing an electric plant—you can either document them or use them as backgrounds for a fiction film. No matter if your film describes the change in a landscape brought about by the cutting of timber, the building of a plant, or simply how someone makes a living, it will interest your audience as long as you yourself are interested.

### Teaching

Anyone who has done even a little teaching knows how valuable films are to education. But instead of borrowing movies from a library, it might be a good

"AU PAYS DE SYLVIE" (Georges Régnier, 1943). — Perhaps you have read "Sylvie," the melancholy story by Gerard de Nerval which takes place in the province of Valois, near Paris. We wanted to bring to life again the poet in his romantic costume, the charming Sylvie, the donkey of the story, and the little laughing boy who led him by the bridle. *(Photo by Célia Films)*

idea to have your class make its own film—perhaps on a science subject. Teachers have guided their pupils in making films even about poetry—or perhaps I should say particularly about poetry. Making a film about the seasons or the life of an animal will teach children to learn by looking—and by doing.

Have a community problem with your schools? People against building more schools? Or don't understand what schools do? Use film making to get your point over.

Perhaps one of the best possible film makers is a doctor. If you are one, think about the trials of getting up at 3 a.m. and going out on call, of the problems of the people you deal with, of the research you may be doing. These are all subjects for films.

## Humor in Amateur Films

This is something that everyone—amateur and professional—should approach with caution. Humor is a delicate thing—hard to create and difficult to sustain. Done well, it contains a balance of observation and irony. Humor, its situations and gestures, are drawn from life. You make them funny by exaggeration. Your job as a film maker is to show the absurdity of the situation—the fettish, the occurence, the prejudice. Humor ranges from the slightly amusing

**THE SOUL OF THE FILM.** — The camera reproduces not only those things which we see, it is also an instrument to link together the images of the world around us and those secret images which are within us. *(Photo by Neubauer)*

to the grotesque. While amateurs have not occupied themselves to any great extent with humor, they really should. A film based on humor requires little in the way of props or elaborate production techniques. Instead the premium is on inventiveness and personal creativity. Seriousness seems to be a sign of the times. But even though one doesn't hear of or see many of the old slap stick type of comedy—one does laugh long and loud when they are shown.

You don't have to go far for the search of comedy. The catastrophic day in the country or the do-it-yourselfer in trouble fit the conditions under which small amateur groups work. Comedy is not a minor film category. Making people laugh isn't easy since a visual joke is a matter of split second timing. You can find some great examples of comedy in many film libraries. It might be a good idea to take a look before starting your own project.

### Poetic Films

One of the miracles of films as a creative tool is that they can express irony, bitterness—and poetry. You may be interested in investigating the nature of man rather than the materialistic things that surround him. The natural world is an endless source of material for those who understand it. In making the nature film, you become part of it. You may be concerned with nature on the grand scale—canyons and scenics—or on the miniscule level—flowers, a rain drop, a leaf, or a tiny bug. All you need is a theme around which to organize your images. It can be your own, one suggested to you by a poem, a book, or a bit of music. Using a few Debussy piano pieces, producer Jean Mitry made a film composed of impressions of a river's reflections.

### Animation

The one outstanding virtue that animation requires is patience. The most familiar animated subject is the cartoon. Each frame of the cartoon film requires a change in a drawing. It may take thousands of drawings to complete a film— thus the need for patience as you shoot one frame at a time.

Animation (or more rightfully, stop motion) can be applied to dolls, toys, puppets, or almost any object. Or, you can go as far afield as Len Lye or Norman McLaren who actually draw and paint on film, working with one frame at a time. They use knives, pointed instruments, what have you, to create a world of almost completely abstract design.

In the final analysis, the wonderful thing about amateur movie making is that with a few rolls of film, a camera, and an idea, you can create a world that perhaps Alice never dreamed existed. It may be the world around you or something that springs from your own mind and being. It may be that amateur movie making serves only to preserve a memory—a place, someone you love. But even for that it is the pure magic of cinema that does it.

The making of a film can satisfy the urge to create. If this book has served to open the door to a new way of life with your motion picture camera, it has served its purpose.